Authentic
Relationships:
being real in an artificial world

Bible Study That Builds Christian Community

LifeWay | Small Groups

LIFE
CONNECTIONS*
BY SERENDIPITY HOUSE

Authentic Relationships: Being Real in an Artificial World
Group Member Book
© 2001, 2003 Serendipity House
Fourth printing 2010

Published by Serendipity House Publishers
Nashville, Tennessee

ISBN: 978-1-5749-4067-1
Item 001208798

Dewey Decimal Classification: 302
Subject Headings: FRIENDSHIP \ DOMESTIC RELATIONS \ INTERPERSONAL RELATIONS

Unless otherwise indicated, all Scripture quotations are from the Holy Bible, New International Version, copyright © 1973, 1978, 1984 by International Bible Society. Used by permission.

To purchase additional copies of this resource or other studies:
ORDER ONLINE at www.SerendipityHouse.com;
WRITE Serendipity House; One LifeWay Plaza; Nashville, TN 37234-0175
FAX (615) 251-5933
PHONE (800) 458-2772

1-800-458-2772
www.SerendipityHouse.com

Printed in the United States of America

Contents

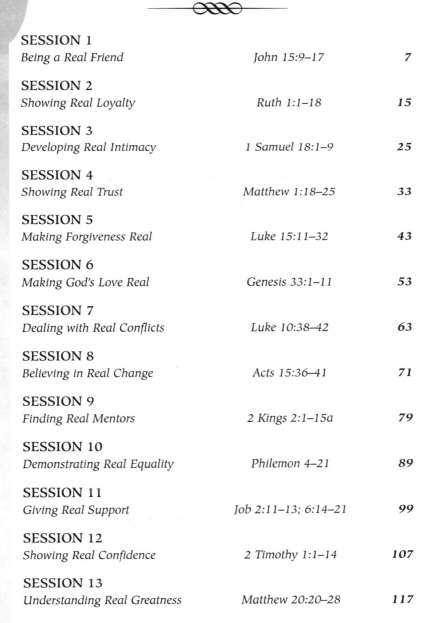

Core Values

Community: The purpose of this curriculum is to build community within the body of believers around Jesus Christ.

Group Process: To build community, the curriculum must be designed to take a group through a step-by-step process of sharing your story with one another.

Interactive Bible Study: To share your "story," the approach to Scripture in the curriculum needs to be open-ended and right-brained—to "level the playing field" and encourage everyone to share.

Developmental Stages: To provide a healthy program in the life cycle of a group, the curriculum needs to offer courses on three levels of commitment:

(1) Beginner Level—low-level entry, high structure, to level the playing field;

(2) Growth Level—deeper Bible study, flexible structure, to encourage group accountability;

(3) Discipleship Level—in-depth Bible study, open structure, to move the group into high gear.

Target Audiences: To build community throughout the culture of the church, the curriculum needs to be flexible, adaptable, and transferable into the structure of the average church.

Mission: To expand the kingdom of God one person at a time by filling the "empty chair." (We add an extra chair to each group session to remind us of our mission.)

Group Covenant

It is important that your group covenant together, agreeing to live out important group values. Once these values are agreed upon, your group will be on its way to experiencing Christian community. It's very important that your group discuss these values—preferably as you begin this study. The first session would be most appropriate. (Check the rules to which each member of your group agrees.)

- [ ] **Priority:** While you are in this course of study, you give the group meetings priority.
- [ ] **Participation:** Everyone is encouraged to participate and no one dominates.
- [ ] **Respect:** Everyone is given the right to his or her own opinion, and all questions are encouraged and respected.
- [ ] **Confidentiality:** Anything that is said in the meeting is never repeated outside the meeting.
- [ ] **Life Change:** We will regularly assess our own life-change goals and encourage one another in our pursuit of Christlikeness.
- [ ] **Empty Chair:** The group stays open to reaching new people at every meeting.
- [ ] **Care and Support:** Permission is given to call upon each other at any time, especially in times of crisis. The group will provide care for every member.
- [ ] **Accountability:** We agree to let the members of the group hold us accountable to the commitments we make in whatever loving ways we decide upon.
- [ ] **Mission:** We will do everything in our power to start a new group.
- [ ] **Ministry:** The group will encourage one another to volunteer and serve in a ministry and to support missions by giving financially and/or personally serving.

notes

Session

1

Being a Real Friend

Prepare for the Session

	READINGS	REFLECTIVE QUESTIONS
Monday	John 15:9	Reflect on how Christ has shown His love to you in the past week.
Tuesday	John 15:10	What command of Christ do you need to focus more on obeying?
Wednesday	John 15:11	In what way has your faith in Christ brought you joy?
Thursday	John 15:12–13	What have you sacrificed for your friends?
Friday	John 15:15	Reflect on what it means to you that Jesus is your friend and how you can open yourself more to that friendship.
Saturday	John 15:16	What kind of "fruit" is your life bearing right now?
Sunday	John 15:16–17	What do you need to ask for in Christ's name to strengthen your friendships?

BIBLE STUDY
- to learn what Jesus meant when He said that we are His friends
- to understand what Jesus' example of friendship means for us in our friendships
- to enumerate some behaviors that help build friendship

LIFE CHANGE
- to set aside at least three hours this coming week for friendship building
- to share something new about ourselves with a friend
- to identify at least two talents a friend has and encourage him or her in at least one of them

Icebreaker
10–15 minutes

Childhood Superheroes. Go around on question 1 and let everyone share a personal hero. Then go around on question 2.

1. Which of the following heroes or superheroes did you most admire and want to be like when you were a child?

- ☐ Superman
- ☐ Nancy Drew
- ☐ Martin Luther King, Jr.
- ☐ Princess Leia (*Star Wars*)
- ☐ Teenage Mutant Ninja Turtles
- ☐ Amelia Earhart
- ☐ Wonder Woman
- ☐ Batman
- ☐ Mother Teresa
- ☐ Zorro
- ☐ Bruce Lee
- ☐ Other:_____

2. What special ability or "superpower" could you most use in your life right now?

- ☐ x-ray vision—to keep track of my child … or mate!
- ☐ the ability to fly—the ultimate escape mechanism!
- ☐ the ability to appear at the crucial moment—to make sure I'm always there to "save the day"!
- ☐ the investigative power of a great detective—to get past the "stories" to the truth
- ☐ invulnerability—so the criticisms of others would bounce off, like bullets bounce off Superman
- ☐ the ability to walk on water—to stay above it all!
- ☐ other: _____

Bible Study

30-45 minutes

The Scripture for this week:

LEARNING FROM THE BIBLE

JOHN 15:9–17

9"As the Father has loved me, so have I loved you. Now remain in my love. 10If you obey my commands, you will remain in my love, just as I have obeyed my Father's commands and remain in his love. 11I have told you this so that my joy may be in you and that your joy may be complete. 12My command is this: Love each other as I have loved you. 13Greater love has no one than this, that he lay down his life for his friends. 14You are my friends if you do what I command. 15I no longer call you servants, because a servant does not know his master's business. Instead, I have called you friends, for everything that I learned from my Father I have made known to you. 16You did not choose me, but I chose you and appointed you to go and bear fruit—fruit that will last. Then the Father will give you whatever you ask in my name. 17This is my command: Love each other."

...about today's session

A WORD FROM THE LEADER

Write your answers here.

1. What makes developing friendships difficult today?

2. Do you have a favorite television "friend"? Why are vicarious television friendships inadequate?

Identifying with the Story

♞ **In horseshoe groups of 6–8, explore questions as time allows.**

1. How would you describe the people you called friends in high school?

IDENTIFYING
WITH THE
STORY
(cont'd)

2. What was something these friends knew about you that most other people did not?

3. What is the greatest sacrifice you remember a friend making for you?

today's session

What is God teaching you from this story?

1. Why is Jesus' friendship with us not a typical friendship?

2. What are some examples of Jesus sharing His feelings with His disciples?

_____

_____

_____

_____

_____

3. What is one example of Jesus sharing particularly vital information with His disciples?

4. What is one way we may need to make a sacrifice for a friend?

5. What kind of "fruit" did Jesus want His disciples to have in their lives?

Learning from the Story

In horseshoe groups of 6–8, choose an answer and explain why you chose what you did.

1. Of the things Jesus talks about in this passage, which one is most important to you in a friendship?

   ☐ Friends reveal their true thoughts and feelings to each other (v. 15).

   ☐ Friends respect each other's wishes (vv. 10,14).

   ☐ Friends sacrifice for each other (v. 13).

   ☐ Friends encourage each other to live "fruitful" lives (v. 16).

2. Rank your own situation on the following scales in terms of whether or not you feel you have friends who do each action.

   REVEAL THEIR TRUE THOUGHTS AND FEELINGS TO ME

   1 · 2 · 3 · 4 · 5 · 6 · 7 · 8 · 9 · 10

   Never   Always

   RESPECT MY WISHES

   1 · 2 · 3 · 4 · 5 · 6 · 7 · 8 · 9 · 10

   Never   Always

   SACRIFICE FOR ME

   1 · 2 · 3 · 4 · 5 · 6 · 7 · 8 · 9 · 10

   Never   Always

   ENCOURAGE ME TO USE MY TALENTS AND BE "FRUITFUL"

   1 · 2 · 3 · 4 · 5 · 6 · 7 · 8 · 9 · 10

   Never   Always

3. To be a better friend to others, which of the following do you most need to work on?

   ☐ Revealing my true thoughts and feelings—I'm a private person.

   ☐ Respecting the desires of others—I get focused on my own agenda!

   ☐ Sacrificing for others—I don't give up things easily.

   ☐ Encouraging the talents of my friends—I get jealous of the talents of others.

life change lessons

How can you apply this session to your life?

Write your answers here.

1. What old saying is quoted in the presentation?

2. What ways are suggested for encouraging friends in the use of their talents?

Caring Time

15-20 minutes

CARING TIME

Remain in horseshoe groups of 6–8.

This is the time for developing and expressing your concern for each other. Thank God for the friendship of Jesus and ask for the grace to be a better friend to others. Pray that each group member will be able to fulfill the life change goals discussed today. Pray also for the concerns and requests listed on the Prayer/Praise Report.

Pray specifically for God to guide you to someone to invite next week.

Take turns praying, remembering the requests and concerns that have been shared. If you would like to pray silently, say "Amen" when you have finished your prayer, so the next person will know when to start.

Reference Notes

Use these notes to gain further understanding
of the text as you study on your own.

**JOHN
15:10**

If you obey my commands. Which commands? The commands to love! Jesus had just referred to His "new command" that they love one another (John 13:34; see also 15:12). The other gospels record that Jesus said the two greatest commandments are to love God with all our hearts, minds, and souls, and to love our neighbor as ourselves (Matt. 22:34–40; Mark 12:28–34; Luke 10:25–28).

**JOHN
15:11**

your joy may be complete. Joy that is focused on one's own well-being alone is not complete. Only joy that sees our connection with God and with all God's creatures is complete because it is joy that does not require the other's sadness.

**JOHN
15:13**

Greater love has no one than this. The ultimate example of love was Jesus' own sacrifice on the cross. Some have said this is a narrower concept than the concept that Christ died for all. But the words of verse 14, "You are my friends if you do what I command" mean that the choice lies with us. All have the opportunity to be Christ's friends.

**JOHN
15:15**

servants ... friends. A relationship of servitude is based on power. A relationship of friendship is based on love. Jesus, in His love, has made His followers privy to information normally only shared among colleagues, not between a master and his servants. Still, this friendship is not one of equals, for it is predicated upon obedience on the part of the disciples.

**JOHN
15:16**

You did not choose me, but I chose you. Some have interpreted this to mean that people have no choice in becoming a Christian—Christ chooses us. However, this passage may be seen as nothing more than historical reality about the first disciples—Jesus went out looking for them, as the Gospels make evident (see, for example, Matt. 4:18–22).

bear fruit—fruit that will last. Jesus is promising that what they accomplish through Him won't be transitory; it will be as eternal as God's kingdom.

notes

Showing Real Loyalty

Prepare for the Session

	READINGS	REFLECTIVE QUESTIONS
Monday	Ruth 1:1–10	What should you consider when trying to determine whether or not to end a friendship?
Tuesday	Ruth 1:11–13	What side benefits are you expecting from your friendships?
Wednesday	Ruth 1:14–17	How readily do you interpret statements made by a friend in despair as personal rejection?
Thursday	Ruth 1:16	Are you willing to commit to "going and staying" with a friend in the midst of your other commitments?
Friday	Ruth 1:16	How important is it to you to share faith in God with your friends?
Saturday	Ruth 1:16–17	Reflect on what has separated you from friends in the past, and whether or not you should have let that separate you.
Sunday	Ruth 1:18	Reflect on how determined you are to show and have loyalty in your friendships.

BIBLE STUDY

- to look at the loyalty Ruth showed to Naomi and learn what it means for our relationships
- to reaffirm the importance of commitment in relationships
- to show how loyalty benefits both parties in a relationship

LIFE CHANGE

- to make a list of times when another person stuck by us when it wasn't necessarily to his or her advantage.
- to write out a vow of loyalty to someone we are in a relationship with
- to thank God daily for His faithfulness

Icebreaker

10-15 minutes

Songs of Home. Go around the group on the first question. Then go around on the second question.

1. Which of the following songs best describes your attitude toward your home when you were in high school?

- ☐ "Happiness Is Lubbock, Texas in the Rearview Mirror" (Mac Davis)
- ☐ "House of Love" (Amy Grant)
- ☐ "Thank God, I'm a Country Boy" (John Denver)
- ☐ "Sweet Home Alabama" (Lynyrd Skynyrd)
- ☐ "We Gotta Get Out of This Place" (Beau Brummels)
- ☐ "In the Ghetto" (Elvis Presley)
- ☐ "California Dreamin' " (The Mamas and the Papas)
- ☐ "Be It Ever So Humble ..." (Traditional)
- ☐ "Little Pink Houses" (John Cougar)

2. If you were to sing a song about your childhood, what style of song would it most likely be?

- ☐ the blues—I've definitely paid my dues!
- ☐ country—full of "down-home" values
- ☐ elevator music—BORING!
- ☐ hard rock—full of rebellion

- ☐ classical—full of sophistication
- ☐ gospel—passionately religious
- ☐ folk music—simple and pure
- ☐ other:_____

Information to Remember: In the spaces provided, take note of information you will need as you participate in this group in the weeks to come.

PEOPLE:

1. A person here I don't know yet is:

2. Something I can do to get acquainted with this person is:

EVENTS: An event that is coming up that I want to make sure I am part of is _____. It will be _____ (time) on _____ (date) at _____ (location).

And if I have time, I would also like to be part of _____. It will be _____ (time) on _____ (date) at _____ (location).

Bible Study

30-45 minutes

The Scripture for this week:

LEARNING FROM THE BIBLE

RUTH 1:1–18

[1]*In the days when the judges ruled, there was a famine in the land, and a man from Bethlehem in Judah, together with his wife and two sons, went to live for a while in the country of Moab.* [2]*The man's name was Elimelech, his wife's name Naomi, and the names of his two sons were Mahlon and Kilion. They were Ephrathites from Bethlehem, Judah. And they went to Moab and lived there.*

[3]*Now Elimelech, Naomi's husband, died, and she was left with her two sons.* [4]*They married Moabite women, one named Orpah and the other Ruth. After they had lived there about ten years,* [5]*both Mahlon and Kilion also died, and Naomi was left without her two sons and her husband.*

⁶When she heard in Moab that the Lord had come to the aid of his people by providing food for them, Naomi and her daughters-in-law prepared to return home from there. ⁷With her two daughters-in-law she left the place where she had been living and set out on the road that would take them back to the land of Judah.

⁸Then Naomi said to her two daughters-in-law, "Go back, each of you, to your mother's home. May the Lord show kindness to you, as you have shown to your dead and to me. ⁹May the Lord grant that each of you will find rest in the home of another husband."

Then she kissed them and they wept aloud ¹⁰and said to her, "We will go back with you to your people."

¹¹But Naomi said, "Return home, my daughters. Why would you come with me? Am I going to have any more sons, who could become your husbands? ¹²Return home, my daughters; I am too old to have another husband. Even if I thought there was still hope for me—even if I had a husband tonight and then gave birth to sons—¹³would you wait until they grew up? Would you remain unmarried for them? No, my daughters. It is more bitter for me than for you, because the Lord's hand has gone out against me!"

¹⁴At this they wept again. Then Orpah kissed her mother-in-law good-by, but Ruth clung to her.

¹⁵"Look," said Naomi, "your sister-in-law is going back to her people and her gods. Go back with her."

¹⁶But Ruth replied, "Don't urge me to leave you or to turn back from you. Where you go I will go, and where you stay I will stay. Your people will be my people and your God my God. ¹⁷Where you die I will die, and there I will be buried. May the Lord deal with me, be it ever so severely, if anything but death separates you and me." ¹⁸When Naomi realized that Ruth was determined to go with her, she stopped urging her.

...about today's session

**A WORD
FROM THE
LEADER**

**Write your
answers
here.**

1. What stories or personal examples can you think of where people seemed to fear commitment?

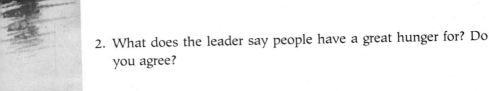

2. What does the leader say people have a great hunger for? Do you agree?

Identifying with the Story

In horseshoe groups of 6–8, explore questions as time allows.

1. Naomi urged her daughters-in-law to go back to their "home." If you could be magically transported back to the place and time in your life that most felt like "home" to you, to what place and time would you go?

2. Who has been most like Naomi to you—a person who, though not a blood relative, you would do almost anything to support if he or she were in need?

3. Who has been most like Ruth to you—the person who has stood by you in your biggest crisis?

today's session

What is God teaching you from this story?

1. What verse in this text is often used in wedding vows? How is that different from its original context?

2. Ruth's loyalty was stronger than what three things?

_____

_____

_____

3. What New Testament example was given for someone feeling a spiritual kinship that is stronger than blood kinship?

4. What other Old Testament books questioned the ethnocentric idea that God was only interested in Israel and wanted foreigners to be shunned?

5. Because of her loyalty, whom did Ruth end up being an ancestor to?

6. Why was Naomi suggesting that Ruth and Orpah go back home?

Learning from the Story

In horseshoe groups of 6–8, choose an answer and explain why you chose what you did.

1. Assuming you did not know how the story ended, what would you have done had you been in Ruth's shoes?

   ☐ I would have been out of there—I don't deal well with poverty!

   ☐ I would have headed home—I'm still my parent's child at heart!

   ☐ I would have been like Orpah—offered to go with Naomi, but relieved to have an out.

   ☐ I would have gone with Naomi—I'm the adventurous type!

   ☐ I would have gone with Naomi—going home is not an attractive option in my case.

   ☐ I would have gone with Naomi—I'm as loyal as the family dog!

   ☐ Other: _____

2. Once you had decided to go with Naomi, what would have been the main focus of your hope for the future?

- ☐ That a good-looking man would come along and save us!
- ☐ Hey, with a real friend by your side you can face anything!
- ☐ I would have figured we needed a miracle of God.
- ☐ I'm not sure I would have had any hope.
- ☐ Other: _____

3. What would you say is the biggest reward for showing loyalty like Ruth did?

- ☐ God's rewards for such behavior—like when He gave Ruth and Boaz to each other.
- ☐ the quality of the friendship that comes out of it
- ☐ if you are loyal to others, others will be loyal to you when you need it
- ☐ just knowing you did the right thing is reward enough
- ☐ other: _____

life change lessons

How can you apply this session to your life?

1. What modern situation might make a person feel like they are in the same situation as Ruth and Naomi were?

Write your answers here.

2. What actions can help motivate us to be loyal in our relationships?

Caring Time

15-20 minutes

During this time, have each group member finish this sentence: "Right now I need a 'Ruth' to stand by me in the midst of … ." Pray for God's guidance and strength in responding to whatever needs are mentioned. Also, use the Prayer/Praise Report and pray for the concerns listed.

Pray specifically for God to guide you to someone to invite next week to fill the empty chair.

Close by thanking God for bringing you together as a group and by asking Him to help you be loyal in your relationships.

Reference Notes

*Use these notes to gain further understanding
of the text as you study on your own.*

In the days when the judges ruled. This was from 1375 B.C. to about 1075 B.C. At the time the Book of Ruth was written it was no longer the case that the judges ruled, so it was probably written in the early years of the kingships. Stories like this would have been passed along carefully by word of mouth. Such story-telling was an art form in the ancient Near East. It is significant that Ruth is placed right after Judges in the Bible. It provides an interesting contrast: Judges chronicled how Israel had *difficulty* showing loyalty to God, while Ruth tells of a foreign woman whose loyalty was exemplary.

there was a famine in the land. Such a famine was also the cause of the migration of Jacob's family to Egypt (see Gen. 42–47).

a man from Bethlehem. This foreshadows one of the central results of this story: Ruth and Boaz were great-grandparents of David (Ruth 4:21–22) and Bethlehem was called the City of David. For Christians, it also reminds us that these were ancestors of Jesus Christ, also born in Bethlehem.

Ephrathites. First Chronicles 2:19–20,50 suggests that Bethlehem was founded by the descendants of a woman named Ephrath, the wife of Caleb.

They married Moabite women. Moab was a traditional enemy of Israel (see especially Numbers 22 and 25). Taking foreign wives was a highly controversial activity for an Israelite. In Deuteronomy 7:1–4 God warns the Israelites not to take foreign wives. Although Moab is not listed there specifically, it is mentioned in 1 Kings 11:1–4, where King Solomon's marriage to foreign women is referred to as a violation of this ban on foreign marriages. In addition, Deuteronomy 23:3 bans Moabites and their descendants down to the tenth generation from entering "the assembly of the Lord." And yet King David was a third generation descendant of a Moabite woman (Ruth 4:21–22)! While there is a mystery in these conflicting reports, it seems evident that God chose this foreign woman to eventually bring to the world the Savior who broke down the dividing walls between Jews and Gentiles (Eph. 2:11–17).

2

left without her two sons and her husband. Women in these times were almost totally dependent on men economically. They could not get a job that paid much. This meant that the plight of these women was desperate indeed.

Go back ... to your mother's home. Generally, women were advised to go back to their "father's house" (see Gen. 38:11; Lev. 22:13). Why is the phrase different here? Perhaps their fathers were dead. Some commentators have suggested that the writer of Ruth was one with a peculiar empathy for the plight and value of women, and this phrase that is unusual for its time might reflect that.

We will go back with you to your people. This first offer would have been the polite thing to do in this culture. Only if they persisted after further insistence that they leave, would this offer to stay with Naomi be thought of as what they really wanted to do. In modern culture, the closest comparison might be when one person at the table in a restaurant offers to pick up the check and the other says, "No, you don't have to do that." Persistence differentiates sincerity from politeness.

any more sons. According to the teaching of Deuteronomy 25:5–6, the brother of a man who died without a son would be obligated to marry his widow and raise up a son for him.

the Lord's hand has gone out. It was assumed in those days that suffering was the result of God's judgment on a person—an assumption that was questioned by the Book of Job. Naomi saw her circumstances as worse than those of Ruth and Orpah because they were young enough to get remarried, while she had little hope for such happening.

Don't urge me to leave you. This well-known saying is often used as part of weddings, but in the original context it is a vow of loyalty from one woman to another.

notes

Session

3

Developing Real Intimacy

Prepare for the Session

	READINGS	REFLECTIVE QUESTIONS
Monday	1 Samuel 18:1–3	Who do you love as much as you love yourself? How do you express your love to that person?
Tuesday	1 Samuel 18:4–5	How generous are you in giving to your friends? What, if anything, holds you back from being more generous?
Wednesday	1 Samuel 18:6–9	How is jealousy interfering with your friendships right now?
Thursday	Proverbs 17:17	In what ways have you become closer to a friend when you have shared adversity?
Friday	Proverbs 18:24	Are you focusing more on developing one or two close friends or a network of mere acquaintances?
Saturday	Proverbs 27:5	Are your friendships based on openness of expression or on hiding who you truly are?
Sunday	Ecclesiastes 4:9–12	Reflect on how you and your friends have supported each other when one of you has fallen.

BIBLE STUDY

· to learn what true intimacy in a relationship means
· to consider the biblical friendship of David and Jonathan as an example of healthy intimacy
· to look at some behaviors that help build intimacy in a relationship

LIFE CHANGE

· to start with our small group in this class and reveal at least one thing about ourselves that we don't normally reveal
· to choose something that we normally would do ourselves and entrust it to a friend
· to give a friend a gift that says something about ourselves

Icebreaker

10-15 minutes

**GATHERING
THE PEOPLE
⋃ Form
horseshoe
groups of 6–8.**

Childhood Jobs. In the family in which you were reared, what jobs were assigned to you? Which one, if any, did you enjoy and which one did you especially dislike? Mark the chores you did with a checkmark (✔), and put an up arrow (⬆) by any job you enjoyed, and a down arrow (⬇) by any job you disliked. Share these with your group.

☐ washing the dishes ☐ taking out the garbage
☐ cleaning my room ☐ doing yard work
☐ doing laundry ☐ helping with a garden
☐ doing farm chores ☐ vacuuming and dusting
☐ helping build or fix things ☐ other:_____
☐ helping care for younger siblings

Information to Remember: In the spaces provided, take note of information you will need as part of this group in the weeks to come.

PEOPLE:

1. A person in the group, besides the leader, I learned from this week was:

2. A person who lifted my spirits was:

EVENTS: An event that is coming up that I want to make sure I am part of is _____. It will be _____ (time) on _____ (date) at _____ (location).

And if I have time, I would also like to be part of _____. It will be _____ (time) on _____ (date) at _____ (location).

Bible Study
30-45 minutes

The Scripture for this week:

[1]*After David had finished talking with Saul, Jonathan became one in spirit with David, and he loved him as himself.* [2]*From that day Saul kept David with him and did not let him return to his father's house.* [3]*And Jonathan made a covenant with David because he loved him as himself.* [4]*Jonathan took off the robe he was wearing and gave it to David, along with his tunic, and even his sword, his bow and his belt.*

[5]*Whatever Saul sent him to do, David did it so successfully that Saul gave him a high rank in the army. This pleased all the people, and Saul's officers as well.*

[6]*When the men were returning home after David had killed the Philistine, the women came out from all the towns of Israel to meet King Saul with singing and dancing, with joyful songs and with tambourines and lutes.* [7]*As they danced, they sang:*

> *"Saul has slain his thousands,*
> *and David his tens of thousands."*

[8]*Saul was very angry; this refrain galled him. "They have credited David with tens of thousands," he thought, "but me with only thousands. What more can he get but the kingdom?"* [9]*And from that time on Saul kept a jealous eye on David.*

**A WORD
FROM THE
LEADER**

**Write your
answers
here.**

1. Why is it inappropriate to just associate intimacy with sexual intercourse?

2. What other biblical men are mentioned who had close friendships? Can you think of others?

Identifying with the Story

♻ **In
horseshoe
groups of 6–8,
explore
questions as
time allows.**

1. As a child or adolescent, what rituals or actions do you remember doing to symbolize a friendship?

   ☐ cutting fingers to become "blood brothers/sisters"
   ☐ exchanging clothes or jewelry
   ☐ developing a special handshake
   ☐ developing a special, exclusive club
   ☐ developing your own special language
   ☐ other: _____

2. When do you remember jealousy threatening or destroying a friendship you had, as it did between David and Saul?

3. If you were to give a friend something right now, something that would symbolize who you are, what might you give?

today's session

1. What was the significance of Jonathan giving David his robe?

2. Why is openness an essential part of having intimate relationships?

3. What was the significance of Jonathan giving David his armor?

4. Why did Saul think Jonathan foolish for not sharing in his suspicion and hostility?

5. What kind of person did the leader say has an easier time trusting? Do you agree or disagree?

6. What did Jonathan do that showed David he could trust him?

Learning from the Story

♘ In horseshoe groups of 6–8, choose an answer and explain why you chose what you did.

1. What is the closest you have come to having a friendship like Jonathan and David had?

2. What is the most important key in developing a friendship like that of David and Jonathan?

☐ there's not much you can do—it's mostly chemistry
☐ work at it—such friendships don't happen overnight
☐ be open—you have to share who you are
☐ trust—you can't feel as if you have to watch your back
☐ be self-giving instead of self-focused—there's no room for big egos in friendship
☐ other: _____

3. What do you need to do to develop more friendships like David and Jonathan's?

☐ take time to work on being a friend
☐ be more open—share more about who I really am
☐ learn to trust again—I've been burned
☐ get my focus off myself
☐ nothing—I'm doing all I can
☐ other: _____

life change lessons

**How can you
apply this
session to
your life?**

**Write your
answers
here.**

1. What should be the approach of someone who doesn't believe he or she can ever have a friendship like David and Jonathan's?

2. When you choose to reveal something new about yourself to someone, what kind of information should you start with?

Caring Time

15-20 minutes

**CARING
TIME**

**◡ Remain
in horseshoe
groups of 6–8.**

Remember that this is the time for expressing your concern for each other and for supporting one another in prayer. Pray specifically that God will help each of you develop the qualities of friendship mentioned in question 2 under "Learning from the Story." Also, pray for the concerns listed on the Prayer/Praise Report.

Pray specifically for God to guide you to someone to invite next week to fill the empty chair.

Close by taking time for each group member to say a brief prayer of thanksgiving for the friendships God has graciously and lovingly given to him or her.

Reference Notes

Use these notes to gain further understanding
of the text as you study on your own.

**1 SAMUEL
18:1**

After David had finished talking with Saul. They had been talking about David's slaying of the Philistine giant, Goliath (see 1 Sam. 17:1–58). *one in spirit.* When Genesis describes the intimacy of marriage, it says husband and wife become "one flesh" (Gen. 2:24). Here the intimacy of friendship is described as being "one in spirit." Others might describe it as being "kindred spirits." There is no indication of what happened to created this sense, only that they "became" one in spirit.

he loved him as himself. Jonathan related to David naturally in the way we are commanded to love others (Lev. 19:18; Matt. 22:34–40; Mark 12:28–34; Luke 10:25–28).

**1 SAMUEL
18:3**

made a covenant. This was a formal, legally binding type of agreement. A covenant was sealed with some kind of sign. The rainbow was the sign of the covenant God made with Noah. Circumcision was a sign of the covenant God made with the people of Israel. The gifts Jonathan gave were a seal of his and David's covenant of friendship.

**1 SAMUEL
18:4**

the robe he was wearing. Clothing in this day indicated your status. This robe would have marked his identity as royalty.

his sword ... his belt. By giving his armor to David, it showed that Jonathan trusted him and was willing to be vulnerable to him.

**1 SAMUEL
18:6**

the women came out. While in many respects women didn't have much value in these times, their praises and songs after a military victory would have been important to the male egos of combatants and generals.

**1 SAMUEL
18:8**

What more can he get but the kingdom? Saul knew that he had displeased God earlier by his disobedience and that God had decided to turn the kingdom over to another (see 1 Sam. 15:1–16:14). No doubt he saw that this was going to happen through David and he sought to avoid this judgment by his acts of violence and jealousy (see 1 Sam. 18:10–16).

notes

4

Showing Real Trust

Prepare for the Session

	READINGS	REFLECTIVE QUESTIONS
Monday	Matthew 1:18–19	What relationship have you considered ending because of a breach of trust?
Tuesday	Matthew 1:20–21	What fear do you need to overcome in order to reach out to those who have hurt you?
Wednesday	Matthew 1:22–23	Reflect on how God has been faithful to His promises in your life.
Thursday	Matthew 1:23–24	How has God been present with you in this past week?
Friday	Matthew 1:24–25	How is God challenging you to be obedient right now?
Saturday	Psalm 56:1–4	How can trusting God help you trust others?
Sunday	Psalm 56:1–4	How are you presently showing your trust in God through your actions?

BIBLE STUDY

· to learn the importance of trust in authentic relationships
· to consider the trust that Joseph showed Mary in relation to her unexpected pregnancy
· to look at some ways to help build trust in a relationship

LIFE CHANGE

· to talk through a strained situation with someone we are having trouble trusting
· to affirm a person who has failed us for a time when he or she *did* come through for us
· to ask a person we are having trouble trusting to do a small task for us

Icebreaker

10-15 minutes

Good Dreams, Bad Dreams. Finish the following sentences to help people know more about you.

1. I know I'm having a bad dream when ...

☐ I'm trapped in a shopping mall—with no credit card!
☐ My actual life seems sane by comparison.
☐ I've lost my respectable job and have become:_____
☐ The sound track is heavy metal.
☐ I'm running around in my "holy" underwear.
☐ I'm being chased by bionic bill collectors.
☐ Other: _____

2. I know I'm having a good dream when ...

☐ I'm trapped in a shopping mall—with unlimited credit!
☐ Julia Roberts (men) or Brad Pitt (women) makes a "guest appearance."
☐ My boss gives me a day off.
☐ My teenagers are actually saying nice things about me.
☐ I realize I have a full week without meetings!
☐ I win the lottery—and I haven't even entered!
☐ Other: _____

Information to Remember: Finish the following sentences as you look around at the people here today.

1. The person in the group with the biggest smile today is:

2. A person who has a look of concern on his or her face, and who I should check on after class is:

Bible Study

30-45 minutes

The Scripture for this week:

**LEARNING
FROM THE
BIBLE**

**MATTHEW
1:18–25**

¹⁸*This is how the birth of Jesus Christ came about: His mother Mary was pledged to be married to Joseph, but before they came together, she was found to be with child through the Holy Spirit.* ¹⁹*Because Joseph her husband was a righteous man and did not want to expose her to public disgrace, he had in mind to divorce her quietly.*

²⁰*But after he had considered this, an angel of the Lord appeared to him in a dream and said, "Joseph son of David, do not be afraid to take Mary home as your wife, because what is conceived in her is from the Holy Spirit.* ²¹*'She will give birth to a son, and you are to give him the name Jesus, because he will save his people from their sins."*

²²*All this took place to fulfill what the Lord had said through the prophet:* ²³*"The virgin will be with child and will give birth to a son, and they will call him Immanuel"—which means, "God with us."*

²⁴*When Joseph woke up, he did what the angel of the Lord had commanded him and took Mary home as his wife.* ²⁵*But he had no union with her until she gave birth to a son. And he gave him the name Jesus.*

A WORD
FROM THE
LEADER

Write your
answers
here.

...about today's session

1. If we want trusting relationships, they have to be
   _____ and _____ ones.

2. Trust also necessitates a willingness to take a _____
   on another person.

Identifying with the Story

U In
horseshoe
groups of 6–8,
explore
questions as
time allows.

1. How did your parents decide what to name you? Does your
   name have any special meaning, and if so, what is it?

2. When have you, like Joseph before his dream of the angel, felt
   like someone you trusted implicitly had betrayed you?

3. What would you have done had you been Joseph and there was
   no angel to tell you the truth of the situation?

   ☐ had Mary stoned
   ☐ started divorce proceedings immediately
   ☐ thought about the possibility of divorce, as Joseph did
   ☐ cried a lot
   ☐ blamed myself for being an inadequate fiancé
   ☐ talked to Mary about it
   ☐ forgiven Mary right away

today's session

1. What three options did Joseph have?

   _____

   _____

   _____

36

2. What were two ways Joseph could have taken revenge on Mary?

_____

_____

3. What does Scripture say about revenge?

4. What problems with revenge are referred to in this session?

_____

_____

_____

4

5. What prophet was called by God to reestablish a relationship with his wife after she committed adultery?

6. What biblical situation is referred to where the people were wise not to trust someone?

7. What three things should we consider in making the choice to trust someone again?

1. _____

2. _____

3. _____

Learning from the Story

☙ In horseshoe groups of 6–8, choose an answer and explain why you chose what you did.

1. The angel told Joseph "do not be afraid" to take Mary as his wife. What do you think he would have been most afraid of prior to this reassurance?

   ☐ that his reputation would suffer—people would think the child was his

   ☐ that people would think he was weak for letting his fiancé do this to him without penalty

   ☐ that he couldn't ever trust Mary again

   ☐ that Mary didn't love him

   ☐ other: _____

2. In what kinds of relationships do you have the hardest time trusting others?

   ☐ in romantic love relationships, like with Joseph

   ☐ in my relationship with my teenage child(ren)

   ☐ in my relationship with my boss and coworkers

   ☐ in groups like this one

   ☐ other: _____

3. What is it that makes you most afraid of trusting?

   ☐ the fear of being made a fool

   ☐ the fear of emotionally investing in someone who will leave me

   ☐ the fear of being taken advantage of financially

   ☐ the fear of being taken advantage of emotionally

   ☐ the fear of failing because I trusted the wrong advice

   ☐ other: _____

life change lessons

How can you
apply this
session to
your life?

Write your
answers
here.

1. What can be learned about trusting from the way an athlete recovers after an injury?

2. In reestablishing trust, how does it help to affirm someone for a time when he or she came through for you?

4

Caring Time

15-20 minutes

CARING
TIME

♡ Remain
in horseshoe
groups of 6–8.

Close by taking time to pray for one another and for your own special concerns. During this time, pray for the ability to trust in the relationships you mentioned in question 2 under "Learning from the Story." Ask for God's guidance to decide when it is safe to trust. Also, use the Prayer/Praise Report and pray for the requests and concerns listed.

Pray specifically for God to guide you to someone to invite next week to fill the empty chair.

Reference Notes

Use these notes to gain further understanding
of the text as you study on your own.

**MATTHEW
1:18**

pledged to be married. A first-century Jewish marriage had three parts to it: the engagement (this often took place when the couple were children and was usually arranged by a marriage broker); the betrothal (a one-year period in which the couple were considered virtually "married," though they did not have sexual relations); and the marriage. Mary and Joseph were at the second stage in their relationship.

she was found to be with child. The penalty in the Old Testament for sleeping with a woman betrothed to another was death by stoning for both parties (Deut. 22:23–24). By this time, however, the breaking of the engagement was the course that was usually followed.

the Holy Spirit. Both Matthew and Luke made it quite clear that the agent in Jesus' birth was the Holy Spirit (Luke 1:35). In the Old Testament, the Spirit is often pictured as a creative force (Gen. 1:2; Ezek. 37:1-14) and, indeed, here the Spirit is at work bringing salvation to the world (Isa. 11:2; 42:1; 61:1; Joel 2:28).

**MATTHEW
1:19**

According to the Law, Joseph was required to break off his relationship with Mary (Deut. 24:1). However, out of compassion for her he decided not to do this publicly. He would not press charges against her as he had the legal right to do.

her husband. Although the marriage had not yet taken place, a betrothed couple was considered to be husband and wife.

divorce. During betrothal, a divorce was required should either party wish to terminate the relationship.

quietly. To break off his engagement privately he would have needed only two witnesses.

**MATTHEW
1:18**

Luke records the visit of the angel to Mary; Matthew records the angelic visit to Joseph.

**MATTHEW
1:20**

a dream. Dreams were often the means by which God revealed Himself to people. Matthew records four other occasions when dreams were crucial during the birth and childhood of Jesus (2:12–13,19,22).

son of David. The crucial link between Joseph and David is made quite clear by the angel.

take Mary home as your wife. The marriage was completed when the husband took his betrothed from her parents' home, where she lived during

MATTHEW 1:20 (cont'd)	the betrothal, to his own home. Joseph needed to marry Mary in order for Jesus to become his legal son and share his lineage back to David.
MATTHEW 1:21	*gave him the name.* It was necessary for Joseph to name Jesus and thus totally accept him as his son. *Jesus.* A common name. It is the Greek form of the Hebrew name Joshua, which means "God is salvation." His name defines His mission. *he will save his people from their sins.* It would not be his goal to establish a Jewish state in what was then Roman territory. Jesus did not come to be a warrior-messiah who would engage in battle against the oppressors of Israel; He would bring to humanity liberation from a far deeper problem—sin.
MATTHEW 1:22	This is the first of 10 instances where Matthew uses this formula (or one like it) to introduce a quotation from the Old Testament. In this way, Matthew points out the way in which Jesus fulfills Old Testament prophecy.
MATTHEW 1:23	The allusion is to Isaiah 7:14. *God with us.* The presence of God with His people is the climactic promise of God's covenant with Israel (see also Matt. 28:20).
MATTHEW 1:24–25	The marriage was completed, though not consummated, until after the birth of Jesus.

4

notes

5

Making Forgiveness Real

Prepare for the Session

	READINGS	REFLECTIVE QUESTIONS
Monday	Luke 15:11–16	What are you squandering in your life right now?
Tuesday	Luke 15:17–19	When have you realized that you needed someone you thought you could do without?
Wednesday	Luke 15:20–21	Contemplate the joy that was in heaven when you accepted Christ as Savior.
Thursday	Luke 15:22–24	What reunion have you celebrated the most in your life?
Friday	Luke 15:25–30	When have you imprisoned yourself with bitterness?
Saturday	Luke 15:31–32	What would you like to celebrate with your friends?
Sunday	Luke 15:32	Reflect on how Christ has brought new life to you.

BIBLE STUDY

- to look at the forgiveness shown in the parable of the prodigal son and see what it says to us today
- to examine the difficulties we have with showing forgiveness
- to understand how God's forgiveness of us models how we are to forgive each other

LIFE CHANGE

- to make a list of some of the things God has forgiven us for
- to talk about a deep hurt with a caring, trusted friend
- to pray for God's forgiving love to fill us

Icebreaker
10-15 minutes

**GATHERING
THE PEOPLE
◡ Form
horseshoe
groups of 6–8.**

Sharing Errant Childhood Ways. Go around the group on question 1 and let everyone share. Then go around again on question 2.

1. When you were nine years old, what were you most likely to feel guilty about?

☐ not getting my chores done   ☐ shoplifting
☐ not getting my schoolwork done   ☐ smoking
☐ lying to my parents   ☐ playing "doctor"
☐ telling on my friends or siblings   ☐ everything I did!
☐ taking money from my parents' dresser
☐ other:_____

2. If you did something wrong at that age, how would your parents generally find out?

☐ I would have a guilty look on my face.
☐ I would confess.
☐ I did a poor job of concealing evidence.
☐ I don't know—they just knew!
☐ I was a lousy liar.
☐ Someone would tell on me.
☐ They didn't; in fact, they still haven't.

Information to Remember: In the spaces provided, take note of information you will need as part of this group in the weeks to come.

PEOPLE:

1. A person here I would really like to get to know better is:

2. A person in this group who has really been a blessing to me during these sessions is:

EVENTS: An event that is coming up that I want to make sure I am part of is _____. It will be _____ (time) on _____ (date) at _____ (location).

And if I have time, I would also like to be part of _____. It will be _____ (time) on _____ (date) at _____ (location).

Bible Study
30-45 minutes

The Scripture for this week:

LEARNING FROM THE BIBLE

LUKE 15:11–32

[11]Jesus continued: "There was a man who had two sons. [12]The younger one said to his father, 'Father, give me my share of the estate.' So he divided his property between them.

[13]"Not long after that, the younger son got together all he had, set off for a distant country and there squandered his wealth in wild living. [14]After he had spent everything, there was a severe famine in that whole country, and he began to be in need. [15]So he went and hired himself out to a citizen of that country, who sent him to his fields to feed pigs. [16]He longed to fill his stomach with the pods that the pigs were eating, but no one gave him anything.

[17]"When he came to his senses, he said, 'How many of my father's hired men have food to spare, and here I am starving to death! [18]I will set out and go back to my father and say to him: Father, I have sinned against heaven and against you. [19]I am no longer worthy to be called your son; make me like one of your hired men.' [20]So he got up and went to his father.

"But while he was still a long way off, his father saw him and was filled with compassion for him; he ran to his son, threw his arms around him and kissed him.

21"The son said to him, 'Father, I have sinned against heaven and against you. I am no longer worthy to be called your son.'

22"But the father said to his servants, 'Quick! Bring the best robe and put it on him. Put a ring on his finger and sandals on his feet. 23Bring the fattened calf and kill it. Let's have a feast and celebrate. 24For this son of mine was dead and is alive again; he was lost and is found.' So they began to celebrate.

25"Meanwhile, the older son was in the field. When he came near the house, he heard music and dancing. 26So he called one of the servants and asked him what was going on. 27'Your brother has come,' he replied, 'and your father has killed the fattened calf because he has him back safe and sound.'

28"The older brother became angry and refused to go in. So his father went out and pleaded with him. 29But he answered his father, 'Look! All these years I've been slaving for you and never disobeyed your orders. Yet you never gave me even a young goat so I could celebrate with my friends. 30But when this son of yours who has squandered your property with prostitutes comes home, you kill the fattened calf for him!'

31" 'My son,' the father said, 'you are always with me, and everything I have is yours. 32But we had to celebrate and be glad, because this brother of yours was dead and is alive again; he was lost and is found.' "

...about today's session

**A WORD
FROM THE
LEADER**

**Write your
answers
here.**

1. What is forgiveness to be modeled after if it is to be true forgiveness?

2. What does it mean to have "false forgiveness"? Have you ever felt you had been given such "false forgiveness"?

Identifying with the Story

In horseshoe groups of 6–8, explore questions as time allows.

1. Who do you most identify with in this parable?

   ☐ The prodigal—because I also have spent some time partying "in a far country."

   ☐ The father—because I know what it's like to worry about a rebellious child.

   ☐ The elder son—I've always tried to be the "good kid."

   ☐ The slaves—I'm usually the last to be considered in family squabbles.

2. What has been the closest you have come to "hitting rock bottom" in your life?

3. Who in your life, like the father in the parable, has forgiven you when you didn't expect it—or deserve it?

5

today's session

What is God teaching you from this story?

1. Why was it an insult for the younger son to ask for his inheritance early?

2. Why was being reduced to feeding pigs especially humiliating to this young man?

3. What three things did the father significantly not do in relation to his younger son's rebellion?

   1. _____

   2. _____

   3. _____

4. What was the meaning behind each of the gifts the father gives the prodigal upon his return?

   1. The best robe:

   2. The ring:

   3. The sandals:

5. Do you agree that we are only making ourselves miserable when we don't forgive? If so, why then do we refuse to do it?

6. How did the elder son show that he no longer thought of the younger son as his brother?

Learning from the Story

1. When have you felt like something important to you was "squandered"?

2. What would you have done had you been the father in this story?
   - ☐ never let my son leave in the first place
   - ☐ written my son every day while he was away
   - ☐ given my son "the cold shoulder" when he returned
   - ☐ made my son prove he was truly sorry before forgiving him
   - ☐ stayed bitter for a long time
   - ☐ forgiven him readily
   - ☐ felt guilty about neglecting the elder son
   - ☐ other: _____

3. What is your biggest barrier to showing forgiveness like the father showed in this story?
   - ☐ People haven't shown me that kind of forgiveness.
   - ☐ My bitterness over injustices done to me, similar to the elder son's attitude
   - ☐ My own self-pity, which I can't seem to let go of
   - ☐ My fear of people taking advantage of me if I'm too forgiving
   - ☐ There are no barriers; I forgive readily because God forgave me.
   - ☐ Other:_____

life change lessons

1. Why is it important that you talk about how you have been hurt as part of the process of forgiving the person who has hurt you?

2. Why is it important that you pray for God's forgiving love to fill you?

Caring Time
15-20 minutes

CARING TIME

♾ Remain in horseshoe groups of 6–8.

Remember that this time is for developing and expressing your care for each other by sharing any personal prayer requests and praying for each other's needs. Pray that the group member to your right will be able, with God's strength, to overcome any barriers to forgiveness, as mentioned in question 3 under "Learning from the Story." Also, use the Prayer/Praise Report and pray for the concerns listed.

Pray specifically for God to guide you to someone to invite next week to fill the empty chair.

Reference Notes

BIBLE STUDY NOTES

Use these notes to gain further understanding
of the text as you study on your own.

LUKE 15:12

give me my share of the estate. Under Jewish law, the younger of two sons was entitled to receive one-third of the estate upon his father's death (Deut. 21:17). While a father might divide up his property before he died if he wished, this son's request would be considered unbelievably callous and hard-hearted. In essence, he is saying that the fact his father was still alive was getting in the way of his plans. The father was under no obligation whatsoever to grant this request; the audience of the day would expect a father faced with such an insulting request to respond with anger. Instead, this father goes along with the request and gives his son the lawful inheritance.

49

got together all he had. In other words, the younger son sold off his share of the estate so that he could have cold, hard cash to do with as he wanted! Such an action would have been scandalous at a time when a person's identity and future were tied up with his family's land. For the sake of satisfying immediate pleasures, he separated himself from his family, threw away his means of income, and robbed any children he may have in the future of the security of owning land.

**LUKE
15:15**

hired himself out … to feed pigs. Jews considered pigs to be ceremonially unclean animals (Lev. 11:7) and would not eat, raise, or touch them. There was even the pronouncement of a curse upon the person who cared for them.

**LUKE
15:16**

He longed to fill his stomach with the pods that the pigs were eating. While eating the food of pigs sounds terrible even to modern readers, for the Pharisees in this audience it would have been utterly horrifying. Jesus painted a picture of an unbelievably arrogant, unpleasant, immoral, foolish, and irreligious young man.

**LUKE
15:19**

no longer worthy to be called your son. The son realized that he had no legal, moral, or relational claim on his father's goodwill.
hired men. These were day laborers employed only as the day-to-day work of the estate demanded.

**LUKE
15:20**

Just as the actions of the son scandalized the Pharisees, so the response of the father violated their understanding of how such a son should be treated.
his father saw him. The implication is that the father had been waiting and hoping to one day see his son return.
was filled with compassion. There is no haughtiness of wounded pride, but only the welling up of pity, love, and joy.
ran to his son. Protocol and dignity were thrown to the wind as the father raced to his son. Social customs dictated that it was degrading for an elderly man to run to anyone, especially to someone who had disgraced him. This picture presents an absolutely unique, staggering insight into the response of the Almighty Holy God to a repentant sinner.
kissed him. While this was a typical greeting for men, it would have been thought inappropriate, given the son's grave offense against his father.

**LUKE
15:21**

I am no longer worthy to be called your son. Although the son may have thought he could earn his way back into some relationship with his father in order to alleviate his own misery, at this point he reflected a true sense of repentance: He could offer nothing except a contrite spirit (Ps. 51:17).

**LUKE
15:22**

the best robe. This would have been the father's best robe. This is a sign that people should honor the son as they honor the father.

LUKE 15:22 (cont'd) *a ring.* The signet ring gave the son the authority to represent the father. *sandals.* Being shoeless was a sign of a slave. To wear shoes indicated a man was free to go where he pleased. Thus, the son was immediately and unconditionally elevated to a position of honor and respect in the home.

LUKE 15:23 *fattened calf.* The fact that it was a calf that was prepared indicates that the whole village was invited to come to the feast (such provisions could feed 100 people).

LUKE 15:24 *was dead.* It was as if the son was dead (he apparently had no intention to live in relationship with his father ever again).

LUKE 15:28 The older son could only see that his father had violated all the customs of how such a wayward son should be treated. His refusal to enter the house would have been seen as a sign of grave disrespect, since the eldest son was expected to play the part of a gracious host at a family feast. As he did with the younger son, the father went out to plead with the older son. This, too, was an overwhelming display of grace since the son's refusal to come to the party was a serious social insult. The parable's listeners would have expected the father to be enraged.

5

LUKE 15:29 *Look!* This would have been considered an extremely rude way for a son to address his father, since there is no hint of respect or affection.

I've been slaving for you. Ironically, this son viewed his ongoing relationship with his father in the way the younger son hoped he might be privileged to have on his return. While always in the vicinity of the father, the older son never enjoyed the relationship with his father that was available to him.

never disobeyed your orders. While there was the appearance of cooperation with the father, this son apparently viewed things in terms of a master/slave relationship. This reflected the Pharisees' reliance upon external conformity to God's law as the measure by which one could earn His blessing.

you never gave me. This observation ignores the fact that he had always been in the position to enjoy the love of his father, whereas the younger son had not.

LUKE 15:31–32 We are not told what the older son did. Jesus left the story open-ended to force the Pharisees to fill in the ending by their behavior.

notes

6

Making God's Love Real

Prepare for the Session

	READINGS	REFLECTIVE QUESTIONS
Monday	Genesis 33:1–4	Over what kinds of issues have you wept with a brother or sister?
Tuesday	Genesis 33:5–7	Reflect on what God has graciously given you.
Wednesday	Genesis 33:8–9	What kinds of things are you doing to gain favor with your friends?
Thursday	Genesis 33:8–9	What kinds of things are you doing to try to find favor with God?
Friday	Genesis 33:10–11	Reflect on what it would be like for you to be face-to-face with the living God.
Saturday	1 John 4:12	How can you show someone God's love today?
Sunday	1 John 4:20	What person or persons are you having the hardest time loving right now?

BIBLE STUDY
- to learn how Jacob experienced God's love in his brother Esau
- to explore the role of forgiveness in experiencing God's love
- to understand what it means to experience God in each other

LIFE CHANGE
- to take the initiative toward reconciliation of a conflict with someone before our next worship experience
- to seek reconciliation between ourselves and a family member, if there are old hurts by calling, writing, or emailing
- to fill ourselves with the biblical passages that urge forgiveness

lcebreaker

10-15 minutes

Family Feud. Go around the group on question 1 and let everyone share. Then go around again on question 2.

1. When you were in grade school, what were the disagreements in your family most likely to be over?

   ☐ who was supposed to do what chores
   ☐ money (between my parents) or my allowance
   ☐ the friends we chose
   ☐ what we watched on television
   ☐ whether we (the children) went to church
   ☐ everything!
   ☐ nothing—we seldom fought!

2. What was the most important thing you learned about resolving family conflicts from these disagreements?

- ☐ Always talk it out.
- ☐ "If you can't say something good, don't say anything at all."
- ☐ Blaming others gets you nowhere.
- ☐ When things get too hot, it's best to just leave.
- ☐ Avoid violence at all costs.
- ☐ Prayer and forgiveness mend a lot of fences.
- ☐ Other:_____

Information to Remember: In the spaces provided, take note of information you will need as part of this group in the weeks to come.

PEOPLE:

1. A person in the group I would like to hear from more today is:

2. A person in the group God may be leading me to say something special to today is:

6

EVENTS: An event that is coming up that I want to make sure I am part of is _____. It will be _____ (time) on _____ (date) at _____ (location).

And if I have time, I would also like to be part of _____.
It will be _____ (time) on _____ (date) at _____ (location).

Bible Study

The Scripture for this week:

¹*Jacob looked up and there was Esau, coming with his four hundred men; so he divided the children among Leah, Rachel and the two maidservants.* ²*He put the maidservants and their children in front, Leah and her children next, and Rachel and Joseph in the rear.* ³*He himself went on ahead and bowed down to the ground seven times as he approached his brother.*

⁴*But Esau ran to meet Jacob and embraced him; he threw his arms around his neck and kissed him. And they wept.* ⁵*Then Esau looked up and saw the women and children. "Who are these with you?" he asked.*

Jacob answered, "They are the children God has graciously given your servant."

⁶*Then the maidservants and their children approached and bowed down.* ⁷*Next, Leah and her children came and bowed down. Last of all came Joseph and Rachel, and they too bowed down.*

⁸*Esau asked, "What do you mean by all these droves I met?"*

"To find favor in your eyes, my lord," he said.

⁹*But Esau said, "I already have plenty, my brother. Keep what you have for yourself."*

¹⁰*"No, please!" said Jacob. "If I have found favor in your eyes, accept this gift from me. For to see your face is like seeing the face of God, now that you have received me favorably.* ¹¹*Please accept the present that was brought to you, for God has been gracious to me and I have all I need." And because Jacob insisted, Esau accepted it.*

...about today's session

A WORD
FROM THE
LEADER

Write your
answers
here.

1. Finish this sentence: "Relating authentically to God seems to require _____ _____."

2. What did it mean that Jacob was renamed "Israel"?

Identifying with the Story

In
horseshoe
ups of 6–8,
explore
uestions as
time allows.

1. When you were a child or adolescent, what was the worst fight you remember having with a sibling or relative of approximately your age?

6

2. When you are feeling guilty about something you have done to someone, which of the tactics used by Jacob are you most likely to use?

☐ sending the person gifts
☐ sending an intermediary ahead to speak for me
☐ "kissing up" to that person, saying nice things about him or her
☐ just talking to them
☐ other:_____

3. If you could go to someone from your past right now to make amends, who would it be?

today's session

What is God teaching you from this story?

1. What did Jacob call the place where he wrestled with an angel, and why did he choose that name?

2. What had Jacob done that gave Esau a right to be angry with him?

3. What are some of the things we do when we expect to meet an angry God?

4. What did Jacob say when he realized Esau had forgiven him?

5. What famous early church leader also learned that finding the love of God often goes hand-in-hand with learning what it means to be loved by another person?

6. Two meanings we can draw from this session are:

   1. _____

   2. _____

Learning from the Story

In horseshoe groups of 6–8, choose an answer and explain why you chose that you did.

1. Which of the following do you think was most important in achieving the reconciliation between Jacob and Esau?

   ☐ Jacob's willingness to humble himself.
   ☐ Esau's success in spite of what Jacob had done to him.
   ☐ Time—it heals all wounds!
   ☐ Esau's love for his brother.
   ☐ God had healed Esau's inner wounds.

2. How do you think this event affected Jacob and Esau's future relationship?

   ☐ It was probably just a temporary respite in a lifetime of fighting.
   ☐ It gave them a good feeling about their relationship to hold onto when they were apart.
   ☐ It made for a more positive, caring relationship.
   ☐ Jacob probably "did Esau some more dirt" just because he knew he could get away with it.
   ☐ Other:_____

3. Jacob told Esau that seeing his face was like seeing the face of God, since he treated Jacob so well. When have you recently felt you experienced God's presence and love through the way someone treated you?

6

life change lessons

How can you apply this session to your life?

Write your answers here.

1. In what passage does Jesus urge us to leave a worship experience to go and find reconciliation with our brother or sister?

2. What are some other passages that urge forgiveness?

Caring Time

15-20 minutes

CARING TIME

♘ **Remain in horseshoe groups of 6–8.**

Close by praying for one another. During this time, thank God for the people through whom group members have experienced God. In addition, pray for the concerns on the Prayer/Praise Report.

Pray specifically for God to guide you to someone to invite next week to fill the empty chair.

Conclude your prayer time by reading together the words of Jesus in John 17:25–26:

> *"Righteous Father, though the world does not know you, I know you, and they know that you have sent me. I have made you known to them, and will continue to make you known in order that the love you have for me may be in them and that I myself may be in them."*

Reference Notes

Use these notes to gain further understanding
of the text as you study on your own.

**GENESIS
33:1–2**

there was Esau. This was the first time Jacob had seen Esau since he had tricked him out of his blessing and birthright, both of which were considered vital to a person's success in the culture of the time. Esau had vowed to kill Jacob in revenge after this incident (see Gen. 27:41).

with his four hundred men. In this time before Israel had a national identity and army, local landowners and persons of prominence had armies of their own, consisting largely of family, friends, and hired help.

divided the children. Jacob had children by two wives, Leah and Rachel, as well as by his maidservants. In the culture of the time, when women were considered to be possessions (the wealthier you were, the more you possessed), this was considered acceptable behavior. Rachel was Jacob's most prized wife, and Joseph his most prized child. Jacob probably put them last to provide them the greatest protection in case Esau attacked.

**GENESIS
33:3**

bowed down to the ground seven times. Seven was a number that indicated perfection or completion. God completed creation in seven days. Here this act may indicate complete contrition. Similar acts of contrition and humility included Jacob's referring to Esau as "lord" (v. 8), and referring to himself as Esau's "servant" (v. 5).

**GENESIS
33:4**

ran to meet Jacob. This scene is reminiscent of the story of the prodigal son, where the father ran to meet his son (see Luke 15:11–32).

kissed him. This was a typical way for men who cared about each other to exchange greetings.

**GENESIS
33:8**

all these droves. Jacob had sent some animals ahead as a gift to try to appease Esau (see Gen. 32:13–16).

**GENESIS
33:10**

like seeing the face of God. Just prior to this story, Jacob had been alone and had wrestled with what he later learned was an angel of the Lord. He named the place where this happened "Peniel" (meaning "face of God") because he felt he had seen God face-to-face. The experience of being loved and forgiven by his brother was on a par with that experience!

6

notes

7

Dealing with Real Conflicts

Prepare for the Session

	READINGS	REFLECTIVE QUESTIONS
Monday	Luke 10:38	How often do you open your home to your brothers and sisters in Christ?
Tuesday	Luke 10:39	What time do you set aside to sit and listen "at the Lord's feet"?
Wednesday	Luke 10:40	What responsibilities are distracting you right now from working on your spiritual growth?
Thursday	Luke 10:40–42	What would Christ say to you about the conflicts you are in right now with those around you?
Friday	Luke 10:41–42	What would Christ say to you about how well you are focusing on the "one thing [that] is needed"?
Saturday	Matthew 18:15	Who do you need to talk to right now about a conflict that has arisen?
Sunday	Matthew 18:16–17	Have you tried everything possible to get that person in conflict with you to listen?

7

BIBLE STUDY
- to examine a conflict between Mary and Martha and see what light it throws on our own conflicts
- to consider what it means to take our conflicts to Jesus
- to learn to verbalize our needs in conflict situations

LIFE CHANGE
- to discuss with the pastor how conflict between members is handled in our church
- to list anyone with whom we have a conflict and with whom we haven't talked directly about that conflict
- to pray about our conflict situation

Icebreaker

10-15 minutes

GATHERING THE PEOPLE ♘ Form horseshoe groups of 6–8.

Clean Freak? Take the following test to help your group determine whether or not you are a "clean freak":

1. If it were totally up to you, would your house look like:

. . . .

a museum set prepared   someone was having a garage
for an open house   sale at a haunted house

2. If we were to look at your desk at home or at your office, would we be more likely to find:

. . . .

everything filed away   a paper avalanche with maybe
or in neat piles   an old sandwich or candy wrapper

3. When you watch reruns of *The Odd Couple* (movie or series) are you more likely to identify with:

. . . .

Felix the neat freak   Oscar the slob

Information to Remember: Finish the following sentences as you look around at the people here today.

1. A person here I would like to hear from more today is:

2. A person in the group who God may be leading me to say something special to today is:

Bible Study

30-45 minutes

The Scripture for this week:

LEARNING FROM THE BIBLE

LUKE 10:38–42

³⁸*As Jesus and his disciples were on their way, he came to a village where a woman named Martha opened her home to him.* ³⁹*She had a sister called Mary, who sat at the Lord's feet listening to what he said.* ⁴⁰*But Martha was distracted by all the preparations that had to be made. She came to him and asked, "Lord, don't you care that my sister has left me to do the work by myself? Tell her to help me!"*

⁴¹*"Martha, Martha," the Lord answered, "you are worried and upset about many things,* ⁴²*but only one thing is needed. Mary has chosen what is better, and it will not be taken away from her."*

7

...about today's session

A WORD FROM THE LEADER

Write your answers here.

1. What does the leader say we applaud in the abstract but have difficulty with in real relationships? Do you agree or disagree?

2. In what area of life do you have the biggest problem with differences: Man/woman relationships? Cultural differences? Age group differences?

Identifying with the Story

1. Which of the following most reminds you of this story about Mary and Martha?

   ☐ My relationship with my siblings when I was an adolescent—we fought over chores.

   ☐ My relationship with my spouse right now—we have different cleaning priorities!

   ☐ Holiday gatherings when the family comes back together as adults—one person ends up doing the work while the others have the fun.

   ☐ Church suppers—the clean-up crew misses the program!

   ☐ Other:_____

2. When you thought something was unfair as a child or adolescent, to whom did you go to rectify things?

3. What are you most likely to get into a conflict about with your friends or family members today?

   ☐ issues of cleanliness and order, like in this story

   ☐ issues of who takes responsibility to get things done, like in this story

   ☐ issues relating to what we do together

   ☐ political or religious beliefs

   ☐ who is in control

   ☐ other:_____

today's session

1. What examples are given of personal conflicts that occurred when Jesus was around?

2. Why is it naive to think that the church won't have conflicts?

3. What are two values that Martha seems to have assumed in her conflict with Mary?

1. _____

2. _____

4. Why should we go first to the person with whom we have the conflict?

5. What did Martha need to learn from her conflict with Mary?

6. What Bible passage advises the option of yielding to the other person in a conflict situation?

7. What should we always do before deciding which option to take in a conflict situation?

7

Learning from the Story

In horseshoe groups of 6–8, choose an answer and explain why you chose what you did.

1. What surprises you most about this story?

- ☐ that in some respects people's behavior hasn't changed much in 2000 years
- ☐ that Jesus seemed to side with a "slacker"!
- ☐ that there was apparently no man in this house
- ☐ that someone could really think about cooking and cleaning with Jesus in the house teaching
- ☐ other:_____

2. How would you summarize Jesus' response to Martha?

- ☐ "Martha, take a chill pill!"
- ☐ "Martha, focus more on your spirit and less on the house."
- ☐ "Just be glad Mary has her spiritual priorities straight."
- ☐ "Martha, you have to learn to put first things first."
- ☐ Other:_____

3. If you had been Martha, what might you have done differently?

- ☐ talked to Mary privately about what needed to be done
- ☐ sat at Jesus' feet along with Mary
- ☐ asked Jesus to hold off teaching until dinner was ready
- ☐ let 'em all starve!
- ☐ just do the work and suffer silently
- ☐ gotten the work done ahead of time so I could sit and listen too
- ☐ I would have done just what Martha did.

life change lessons

How can you apply this session to your life?

1. Who should you talk to about how conflict is handled in your church?

Write your answers here.

2. What should you avoid when talking to someone with whom you have a conflict?

Caring Time

15-20 minutes

CARING TIME

♘ **Remain in horseshoe groups of 6–8.**

Take time now to care for one another through prayer. Go around the group and have each member share one relational conflict they are having where they need direction from God; then have your group pray for those conflicts. Take turns praying for one another, remembering the concerns that have been shared. Also, use the Prayer/Praise Report and pray for the concerns listed.

Pray specifically for God to guide you to someone to invite next week to fill the empty chair.

Close by asking God to give each group member the strength and wisdom to accomplish the life change goals from this session.

Reference Notes

Use these notes to gain further understanding
of the text as you study on your own.

**LUKE
10:38**

village. Bethany, just on the outskirts of Jerusalem, was the home of Martha and Mary and their brother Lazarus (whom Jesus raised from the dead).
a woman named Martha. Martha and Mary also appear in John 11:1–44, where their brother Lazarus died and was resurrected by Jesus. In that story it was Martha, rather than Mary, who was portrayed as the more faithful one.
Martha opened her home to him. It appears that it was Martha's home (she was the head of the household), which explains why she felt more responsibility for the preparations.

**LUKE
10:40**

my sister has left me to do the work by myself. This is a classic clash between a disciplined, task-oriented servant (Martha) and a more impulsive, person-oriented student (Mary). That Martha says Mary has left her to do all the work assumes the priority that work always comes first over learning and socialization. Martha emotionalized the issue by implying that those who don't share her priority "don't care." None of this is to say that Jesus "sided" against the more task-oriented person. He simply said that in this situation, with Jesus Himself present for a brief time, stopping to learn from Him should be the highest priority, and Mary chose that priority.

**LUKE
10:41**

you are worried and upset. Martha was like the thorny soil in which the seed is choked by life's worries (Luke 8:14).
about many things. Martha's problem was an inability to focus her life around one central priority. As a result, she tried to be the "superwoman" who "does it all." Jesus calls us to focus our lives around the central priority of the kingdom of God, which then helps all other tasks and goals find their proper place (Matt. 6:25–34).

**LUKE
10:42**

only one thing is needed. Jesus is saying that listening and responding to the Word of the kingdom is the single most important thing in all of life. Mary had chosen to do that, rather than being distracted with the less important expectations of hospitality. Jesus gently commended that attitude to Martha who, in her zeal to "serve" Jesus, missed the importance of His presence and His words.

notes

Believing in **Real Change**

Prepare for the Session

	READINGS	REFLECTIVE QUESTIONS
Monday	Acts 15:36	What friend or friends do you need to check up on?
Tuesday	Acts 15:37–39	When has a serious disagreement come between you and a friend? Do you still need to work on mending fences?
Wednesday	Acts 15:40	What friend has come into your life to help fill a gap left by the loss of another friend?
Thursday	Acts 15:41	What are you doing now to strengthen your church?
Friday	2 Corinthians 5:17	Reflect on how you have seen Christ change your friends. What were the biggest changes you saw when a friend became a Christian?
Saturday	Romans 7:18–19	Why is it so hard to change in our own power?
Sunday	Romans 7:24-25	How has Christ helped you change the direction of your life?

8

BIBLE STUDY

- to look at the conflict Paul had with Barnabas over Mark and see what it says about the ability of people to change
- to understand how Christ helps change people
- to consider what it means behaviorally to believe that people really can change

LIFE CHANGE

- to make a list of positive changes we have made in your lives over the last 10 years
- to ask God to point us to people He is changing
- to choose one person to entrust with a task at which he or she has previously failed

Icebreaker

10-15 minutes

Responsible Me. Go around the group on question 1 and let everyone share. Then go around again on question 2.

1. Which of the following were you responsible for as a child?

☐ caring for a younger sibling   ☐ yard work
☐ cleaning my room   ☐ farm chores
☐ doing the dishes   ☐ fixing meals
☐ seemingly everything!   ☐ nothing

2. What do you dislike having to be responsible for today?

☐ important decision making in my job
☐ balancing the checkbook
☐ picking up after others
☐ myself!
☐ other people's happiness
☐ other:_____

Information to Remember: Take note of information you will need as part of this group in the weeks to come. Finish the following sentences as you look around at the people here today.

PEOPLE:

1. Someone normally here who is missing this week is:

2. What I can do to help this person know he or she was missed is:

EVENTS: An event that is coming up that I want to make sure I am part of is _____. It will be _____ (time) on _____ (date) at _____ (location).

And if I have time, I would also like to be part of _____. It will be _____ (time) on _____ (date) at _____ (location).

Bible Study

30-45 minutes

The Scripture for this week:

LEARNING FROM THE BIBLE

ACTS 15:36–41

[36]*Some time later Paul said to Barnabas, "Let us go back and visit the brothers in all the towns where we preached the word of the Lord and see how they are doing."* [37]*Barnabas wanted to take John, also called Mark, with them,* [38]*but Paul did not think it wise to take him, because he had deserted them in Pamphylia and had not continued with them in the work.* [39]*They had such a sharp disagreement that they parted company. Barnabas took Mark and sailed for Cyprus,* [40]*but Paul chose Silas and left, commended by the brothers to the grace of the Lord.* [41]*He went through Syria and Cilicia, strengthening the churches.*

8

...about today's session

A WORD FROM THE LEADER

Write your answers here.

1. What people does the leader refer to who seem to doubt the ability of people to change? What similar quotes have you heard?

2. What is the implication of the teaching that if anyone is in Christ he or she is a "new creation" (2 Cor. 5:17)?

Identifying with the Story

1. When you were a child or adolescent, who was a special relative to you—one you had more in common with than anyone else?

2. Who in your past stuck up for you when nobody else would?

3. When have you felt like someone let you down by not following through with a commitment he or she made to you?

today's session

1. Where did John Mark desert Paul and his missionary team?

2. What was John Mark's relationship to Barnabas?

3. What later contributions did John Mark make to the spread of the gospel?

4. What other biblical person is mentioned as an example of people changing?

5. What are two ways Christ breaks our cycles of failure?

    1. _____

    2. _____

6. What biblical reference is given for when Paul wrestled with his own cycle of failure? What cycle of failure did Paul fight?

Learning from the Story

In horseshoe groups of 6–8, choose an answer and explain why you chose what you did.

1. What surprises you most about this story?

   ☐ that Scripture even records such an argument between two famous church leaders

   ☐ that a Christian leader like Paul was unwilling to forgive and forget

   ☐ that Barnabas still trusted Mark after their previous experience

   ☐ that Paul and Barnabas couldn't come to a better compromise

   ☐ other:_____

2. In terms of how you normally act in situations like this one, where a decision needs to be made about trusting someone who has previously failed you, who are you more like?

   1 · 2 · 3 · 4 · 5 · 6 · 7 · 8 · 9 · 10

   Paul—"once bitten, twice shy"   Barnabas—"always believe the best about people!"

8

3. Apparently, John Mark was able to change and stood with Paul in a time of need (Col. 4:10; 2 Tim. 4:11; Philem. 24). What do you see as the most relevant factors in helping a person make that kind of change in his or her life? Rank the following factors from 1 (least relevant) to 5 (most relevant):

___ people like Barnabas, believing in them and standing by them

___ people like Paul, not coddling them but making them reach for a higher standard

___ the maturity that comes with age

___ the power of Jesus Christ in one's life

___ the ability to learn from one's mistakes

life change lessons

1. What comic strip character is referred to as struggling with the question of when to believe if someone has truly changed?

2. What action can help us decide *when* to believe someone has made a real change in his or her life?

Caring Time
15-20 minutes

Take this time to encourage one another in prayer. Have group members take turns answering the question, "In what ways do you feel you need to make a change like John Mark made?" Then have each person pray for the person to his or her left, remembering the changes that were shared. In addition, pray for the concerns on the Prayer/Praise Report.

Pray specifically for God to guide you to someone to invite next week to fill the empty chair.

Reference Notes

Use these notes to gain further understanding
of the text as you study on your own.

**ACTS
15:36**

visit the brothers. Paul was not a "fly-by-night" evangelist who arrived, "converted" people, and then headed on his own way never to be heard from again. He had a deep concern for everyone he brought into the faith and was concerned that they thrive and grow as Christians. This is why he decided to go back and visit them.

**ACTS
15:37**

John, also called Mark. He was the author of the Gospel of Mark and a cousin of Barnabas (Col. 4:10). His mother's home was apparently an important house church in Jerusalem since it was where the disciples met to pray for Peter's release when he was imprisoned (Acts 12:12).

**ACTS
15:38**

he had deserted them. While the word used to describe Mark's leaving in Acts 13:13 is a neutral one that implies nothing negative, the word used here is related to the word for *apostasy*. Luke does not tell us why Mark left, but Paul certainly viewed it as a serious deficit and was unwilling to let him try again.

**ACTS
15:39–40**

a sharp disagreement. This is a strong word used in the Septuagint version of the Old Testament to describe God's anger at the idolatry of Israel (Deut. 29:28; Jer. 32:37). Barnabas' concern may have been motivated in part by the fact that Mark was his cousin (Col. 4:10), but it is characteristic of Barnabas. Years before, it was he who insisted that Paul be given a chance to prove himself to the apostles (Acts 9:27) and recognized Paul's gifts for ministry (Acts 11:25–26). On the other hand, Paul was concerned about the immediate needs and demands of such a rigorous journey. Undoubtedly, Mark's eager departure placed increased demands on Paul and Barnabas, and he was unwilling to risk that again. While the action focuses on Paul and Silas, Barnabas and Mark also left Antioch on a missionary trip as they returned to Cyprus (Acts 13:4–12). Early church tradition teaches that Barnabas remained there until his death. Paul's letters reveal that he and Barnabas were later reconciled (Col. 4:10) and that Mark was counted by Paul as a valuable assistant (Col. 4:10; 2 Tim. 4:11; Philem. 24).

**ACTS
15:39–40**

Whereas the limits of Paul's first journey were reached by an overland trek westward to the border of Cilicia, this time he went east, going overland through the provinces until he came to Derbe (Acts 16:1; see also Acts 14:20). Thus, the last community he visited on his earlier journey was the first to be visited on his second journey.

8

notes

Finding Real Mentors

Prepare for the Session

	READINGS	REFLECTIVE QUESTIONS
Monday	2 Kings 2:1–2	Who can you count on to be by your side at all costs?
Tuesday	2 Kings 2:3–6	How prepared are you for the death of people who are nearest to you?
Wednesday	2 Kings 2:7–8	What "river" blocks the path to where you feel called to go in life?
Thursday	2 Kings 2:8	Who has taught you the most about dealing with the obstacles in your path?
Friday	2 Kings 2:9–10	Reflect on what you expect of your friends.
Saturday	2 Kings 2:11–12	When might God have separated you from a close friend so you could grow?
Sunday	2 Kings 2:13–15a	When has God shown you that He is with you, just as He was with those who have gone before you?

BIBLE STUDY
- to look at the mentoring relationship between Elijah and Elisha and see what example it provides for us
- to learn why mentoring relationships are valuable
- to consider the qualities one should look for in a mentor

LIFE CHANGE

Needing a Mentor:
- to make a list of qualities we need in a mentor
- to go to our pastor and ask if he knows people with the qualities we have listed as important in a mentor
- to choose one person and make an appointment to talk to him or her about mentoring

Ready to Mentor:
- to ask our pastor or a mature Christian who knows us well, whether he or she sees us as qualified to mentor
- to go to our youth minister or whomever works with youth or young adults in our church and ask for names of younger people who need a mentor
- to choose one person and make an appointment to talk to him or her about mentoring

Icebreaker

Spiritual Gifts. Take out your wallet or purse. Find one thing to give (just for the duration of this class!) to the person on your right. It should be something that represents a spiritual quality you would like them to have. Maybe it's a quality that you also need or one that you have learned to develop over your lifetime. Look at the list below for some examples of gifts that might be given. But remember, gift possibilities are not limited to these:

- ✧ a social security card—that you might feel secure in your relationships
- ✧ a mirror—that you will always be able to see the beauty others see in you
- ✧ a pair of glasses—that your eyes might always see the wonders around us
- ✧ a family picture—that you might stay focused on the people who are important to you
- ✧ a set of keys—that God might set before you open doors of opportunity
- ✧ an aspirin or pain reliever—that God might ease the suffering you are going through

Information to Remember: In the spaces provided, take note of information you will need as part of this group in the weeks to come.

9

PEOPLE:

1. A person here I would like to hear more from today is:

2. A person here God may be leading me to say something special to today is:

EVENTS: An event that is coming up that I want to make sure I am part of is _____. It will be _____ (time) on _____ (date) at _____ (location).

And if I have time, I would also like to be part of _____. It will be _____ (time) on _____ (date) at _____ (location).

Bible Study

30-45 minutes

The Scripture for this week:

¹*When the Lord was about to take Elijah up to heaven in a whirlwind, Elijah and Elisha were on their way from Gilgal. ²Elijah said to Elisha, "Stay here; the Lord has sent me to Bethel."*

But Elisha said, "As surely as the Lord lives and as you live, I will not leave you." So they went down to Bethel.

³*The company of the prophets at Bethel came out to Elisha and asked, "Do you know that the Lord is going to take your master from you today?"*

"Yes, I know," Elisha replied, "but do not speak of it."

⁴*Then Elijah said to him, "Stay here, Elisha; the Lord has sent me to Jericho."*

And he replied, "As surely as the Lord lives and as you live, I will not leave you." So they went to Jericho.

⁵*The company of the prophets at Jericho went up to Elisha and asked him, "Do you know that the Lord is going to take your master from you today?"*

"Yes, I know," he replied, "but do not speak of it."

⁶*Then Elijah said to him, "Stay here; the Lord has sent me to the Jordan."*

And he replied, "As surely as the Lord lives and as you live, I will not leave you." So the two of them walked on.

⁷*Fifty men of the company of the prophets went and stood at a distance, facing the place where Elijah and Elisha had stopped at the Jordan. ⁸Elijah took his cloak, rolled it up and struck the water with it. The water divided to the right and to the left, and the two of them crossed over on dry ground.*

⁹When they had crossed, Elijah said to Elisha, "Tell me, what can I do for you before I am taken from you?"

"Let me inherit a double portion of your spirit," Elisha replied.

¹⁰"You have asked a difficult thing," Elijah said, "yet if you see me when I am taken from you, it will be yours—otherwise not."

¹¹As they were walking along and talking together, suddenly a chariot of fire and horses of fire appeared and separated the two of them, and Elijah went up to heaven in a whirlwind. ¹²Elisha saw this and cried out, "My father! My father! The chariots and horsemen of Israel!" And Elisha saw him no more. Then he took hold of his own clothes and tore them apart.

¹³He picked up the cloak that had fallen from Elijah and went back and stood on the bank of the Jordan. ¹⁴Then he took the cloak that had fallen from him and struck the water with it. "Where now is the Lord, the God of Elijah?" he asked. When he struck the water, it divided to the right and to the left, and he crossed over.

¹⁵The company of the prophets from Jericho, who were watching, said, "The spirit of Elijah is resting on Elisha."

...about today's session

A WORD
FROM THE
LEADER

Write your
answers
here.

1. Why are many young people looking for mentors today?

2. Who were some mentors in Scripture?

9

Identifying with the Story

◡ In
horseshoe
groups of 6–8,
explore
questions as
time allows.

1. Whose death affected you the most when you were a child or adolescent?

2. If you could receive "a double portion" of the spirit of any person you have known, who would it be, and why?

3. What skill or ability do you have that you learned or inherited from a parent or mentor?

today's session

1. What were some of Elijah's accomplishments during his career as a prophet?

2. What was Elisha doing when Elijah found him and called him to follow him?

3. What are some factors Fred Smith says we should consider in pairing mentor and mentoree?

    1. _____

    2. _____

    3. _____

    4. _____

    5. _____

4. Of what other biblical character's pledge of commitment does Elijah's pledge remind us?

5. In what other biblical story are we reminded that a mentoring relationship is meant to be a temporary one?

6. What is the main responsibility of the mentor in the mentoring relationship?

Learning from the Story

In horseshoe groups of 6–8, choose an answer and explain why you chose what you did.

1. What surprises you most in this story?
   - [ ] that everyone seems to know what is going to happen to Elijah
   - [ ] that Elijah and Elisha travel so far in one day
   - [ ] that Elijah is able to pass his miraculous power on to Elisha
   - [ ] that Elijah seems to be trying to leave Elisha behind all the time
   - [ ] other:_____

2. What do you see as the most influential factor in Elisha being able to take on the power of Elijah?
   - [ ] his persistence in sticking by Elijah everywhere he went, even being present at his ascent to heaven (v. 11)
   - [ ] his picking up Elijah's cloak (vv. 13–14)
   - [ ] his learning about what it means to follow God's lead (vv. 2,4,6)
   - [ ] other:_____

3. Which of the following do you see as most critical to a mentoring relationship, such as existed between Elijah and Elisha?
   - [ ] loyalty, such as Elisha showed (vv. 2,4,6)
   - [ ] a mentor who truly wants to help the person he or she is mentoring (v. 9)
   - [ ] a love between each other that is like parent and child (v. 12)
   - [ ] the willingness to follow your mentor anywhere (vv. 2,4,6)
   - [ ] the ability of the person mentored to observe the mentor in action (vv. 8,14)

9

life change lessons

How can you apply this session to your life?

Write your answers here.

1. What should be the first action of a person needing a mentor, according to the leader?

2. After hearing this presentation, to whom might you talk to see if you are qualified to be a mentor?

Caring Time

15-20 minutes

CARING TIME

U **Remain in horseshoe groups of 6–8.**

Use this time to pray for one another. Ask for God's discernment and guidance in choosing a mentor or in choosing whether or not to become a mentor. Remember to use the Prayer/Praise Report and pray for the requests and concerns listed.

Pray specifically for God to guide you to someone to invite next week to fill the empty chair.

Close by thanking God for those who have served as mentors to persons in the group.

Reference Notes

BIBLE STUDY NOTES

Use these notes to gain further understanding
of the text as you study on your own.

2 KINGS 2:1

whirlwind. The coming of God is often associated with a strong wind (see Isa. 29:6; 40:24; Ezek. 13:11; Zech. 9:14; Acts 2:1–2).

2 KINGS 2:3

The company of the prophets. The prophets of a given locale were joined in somewhat of a fraternal relationship. All of these, along with prophets at Jericho (v. 5) and probably the Jordan (v. 7), seemed to be aware that Elijah would depart this world in a special way.

2 KINGS 2:8	**The water divided.** This scene is reminiscent of the parting of the Red Sea (Ex. 14:15–31), as well as the crossing of the Jordan when the people of Israel originally entered the promised land (Josh. 3). It would have been seen as an evidence of God's presence with Elijah.
2 KINGS 2:9	**a double portion.** A man's firstborn son received a double portion of his inheritance—twice as much as other sons would receive (see Deut. 21:15–17). This does not mean twice as much as Elijah himself had. While Elisha was not biologically Elijah's son, he was his spiritual son. So what he is asking is not part of Elijah's physical inheritance, but something much more valuable to him—his spiritual inheritance.
2 KINGS 2:10	**if you see me.** This required both Elisha's loyalty, that he stick around until that time, as well as his perception, that he be able to see the spiritual portents, such as the chariots of fire from heaven. Only the spiritually discerning could see such things (see 2 Kings 6:17).
2 KINGS 2:11	**separated the two of them.** Elisha had already shown that he would never voluntarily leave the side of his mentor, and so it took an act of God to separate Elisha from Elijah's side. **Elijah went up to heaven.** The representation here is that Elijah did not actually die, but was taken directly to heaven. While Jewish tradition held the same had been true of Moses, Deuteronomy 34:5 said he actually died. Of no other character in Scripture is it said that he or she went directly to heaven without dying, and this was a tribute to Elijah's great spiritual stature. Because of this special way of departing, it was later said that Elijah would first return as a sign of the coming of the Messiah. Elijah joined Moses to be with Jesus on the Mount of Transfiguration (Matt. 17:1–13).
2 KINGS 2:12	**Elisha saw this.** This fulfilled the requirement put upon him by Elijah in verse 10. **took hold of his own clothes and tore them apart.** This was a sign of mourning.
2 KINGS 2:13	**He picked up the cloak.** Some of the power of such a great man of faith was felt to be transferred to his clothing. We see this again with Jesus when a woman with a hemorrhage decided that if she just touched the hem of Jesus' garment, she would be healed (see Matt. 9:20–21).
2 KINGS 2:14	**Where now is the Lord, the God of Elijah?** One of the drawbacks of having such a great person of faith around is people can get the idea that once that person is gone, God will no longer be able to do great things. Elisha here shows that the God of Elijah is still alive and well! This is reminiscent of how Jesus later said of the one who follows Him, "He will do even greater things than these, because I am going to the Father" (John 14:12).

9

notes

10

Demonstrating Real Equality

Prepare for the Session

	READINGS	REFLECTIVE QUESTIONS
Monday	Philemon 4–5	Who do you especially thank God for right now?
Tuesday	Philemon 6–7	In what ways are you "refreshing the hearts of the saints"?
Wednesday	Philemon 8–11	What friends do you have who are as close or closer to you than family?
Thursday	Philemon 12–16	When has God used separation to make you even closer to a friend or loved one?
Friday	Philemon 17–21	Which of your friends do you feel you owe a favor?
Saturday	Galatians 3:28	What group do you sometimes have trouble seeing your oneness with, even when they are in Christ?
Sunday	James 2:1–4	What do you need to start doing to witness to the truth that we are all equal before God?

10

BIBLE STUDY

· to look at the change in status that occurred in biblical times when slave and owner were brothers in Christ

· to understand what it means that in Christ the person who flips hamburgers has equal status with the corporate CEO

· to discuss the implications of the fact that we are all equals in Christ in how we run our churches

LIFE CHANGE

· to focus this week on sharing a smile and an affirmation with each person we come in contact with in a service profession

· to discuss with three different people in our church, in three different stations in life, how they see God using them

· to listen to one person we are not used to listening to

Icebreaker

10-15 minutes

**GATHERING
THE PEOPLE
◡ Form
horseshoe
groups of 6–8.**

If You're Looking for Me. Go around the group on question 1, letting everyone share an answer, and then do the same with question 2.

1. Choose five of the following pairs and tell which part of the pair says best where you are most likely to be found. Are you more likely to be found:

at McDonald's	at Chez Pierre's
at K-Mart	at Saks Fifth Avenue
at a ball game	at a concert
at a friend's having coffee	at work, making deals
seeking sand and surf	surfing the Internet
finding new places	returning to old places
at a children's program	at a board meeting
tending livestock	investing in the stock market

2. If you don't want to be found, where do you go?

Information to Remember: Finish the following sentences as you look around at the people here today.

1. Someone normally here who is missing this week is:

2. What I can do to help this person know he or she was missed is:

Bible Study

30-45 minutes

The Scripture for this week:

⁴I always thank my God as I remember you in my prayers, ⁵because I hear about your faith in the Lord Jesus and your love for all the saints. ⁶I pray that you may be active in sharing your faith, so that you will have a full understanding of every good thing we have in Christ. ⁷Your love has given me great joy and encouragement, because you, brother, have refreshed the hearts of the saints.

⁸Therefore, although in Christ I could be bold and order you to do what you ought to do, ⁹yet I appeal to you on the basis of love. I then, as Paul—an old man and now also a prisoner of Christ Jesus—¹⁰I appeal to you for my son Onesimus, who became my son while I was in chains. ¹¹Formerly he was useless to you, but now he has become useful both to you and to me.

¹²I am sending him—who is my very heart—back to you. ¹³I would have liked to keep him with me so that he could take your place in helping me while I am in chains for the gospel. ¹⁴But I did not want to do anything without your consent, so that any favor you do will be spontaneous and not forced. ¹⁵Perhaps the reason he was separated from you for a little while was that you might have him back for good—¹⁶no longer as a slave, but better than a slave, as a dear brother. He is very dear to me but even dearer to you, both as a man and as a brother in the Lord.

10

[17]So if you consider me a partner, welcome him as you would welcome me. [18]If he has done you any wrong or owes you anything, charge it to me. [19]I, Paul, am writing this with my own hand. I will pay it back—not to mention that you owe me your very self. [20]I do wish, brother, that I may have some benefit from you in the Lord; refresh my heart in Christ. [21]Confident of your obedience, I write to you, knowing that you will do even more than I ask.

...about today's session

A WORD FROM THE LEADER

Write your answers here.

1. In what ways has our country expanded its vision of what it means that all people are created equal?

2. For our relationships to be _____ Christian, we need to show it not just by our words, but also by our _____ that we realize all people are _____ in the sight of God.

Identifying with the Story

♘ **In horseshoe groups of 6–8, explore questions as time allows.**

1. How many brothers and sisters do you have? Which one are you closest to?

2. Who is like a brother or sister to you? What qualities does this person have that make you see him or her in this way?

3. Which of the following has been most likely to separate you from someone you felt was like a brother or sister to you?

☐ job moves
☐ rivalry over members of the opposite sex
☐ growing in different directions
☐ one of us got married
☐ other:_____

today's session

What is God teaching you from this story?

1. What did the pious Jewish male thank God for in his prayer?

2. What does Paul say in Galatians 3:28 that sums up the change in status that came through Jesus Christ?

3. What three words does the leader refer to as having meaning in relation to the transformation brought about by Christ?

_____

_____

_____

4. Why is having a brother or sister better than having a slave?

10

5. What does the name Onesimus mean in Greek?

6. Where in Scripture does Paul give us a different concept of who we are to be a slave to and what that means?

Learning from the Story

♘ **In
horseshoe
groups of 6–8,
choose an
answer and
explain why
you chose
what you did.**

1. What impression do you get of Paul from how he handles this matter of Onesimus and his relationship to Philemon?

    ☐ He really knew how to pull the guilt strings!
    ☐ He knew how to be a strong advocate for someone else.
    ☐ He believed in the equality of all people.
    ☐ He wasn't a strong advocate for societal change.
    ☐ Other:_____

2. When have you felt someone, whom others might have thought was of a different social status than you, was really a spiritual brother or sister and status, power, or money did not matter?

3. Which of the following factors are most influential in determining who feels like a brother or sister to you?

    ☐ similar interests
    ☐ similar beliefs
    ☐ similar life experiences
    ☐ honest communication
    ☐ sharing the same space together and learning to get along
    ☐ other:_____

life change lessons

ow can you
apply this
session to
your life?

Write your
answers
here.

1. What three examples are given of how our behaviors can show that we don't truly believe all people are of equal worth before God?

_____

_____

_____

2. What does it say to a person when you truly listen to him or her?

Caring Time
15-20 minutes

CARING TIME

☺ **Remain**
horseshoe
oups of 6–8.

Close by sharing prayer requests and praying for one another. Have each person in the group share how someone served him or her in this past week. Pray that all of those people can someday be brothers and sisters in Christ. In addition, pray for the concerns on the Prayer/Praise Report.

Pray specifically for God to guide you to someone to invite next week to fill the empty chair.

10

Reference Notes

Use these notes to gain further understanding
of the text as you study on your own.

**PHILEMON
5**

faith ... love. While Paul often uses some combination of the triad of faith, hope, and love in his letters, the emphasis here falls upon the love God expects to be demonstrated between Christians.

**PHILEMON
6**

sharing your faith. Literally, "your fellowship of the faith." This is not a prayer for fruitfulness of some type of evangelistic activity, but a desire that Philemon's participation in the faith would continue to be actively expressed by his good deeds.

so that you will have a full understanding of every good thing we have in Christ. Participation in Christ requires believers to behave toward others with the same goodness that Christ has shown them.

**PHILEMON
7**

refreshed the hearts. As Philemon has encouraged the hearts of so many others, Paul will appeal to him to "refresh my heart" (v. 20) by receiving Onesimus as a brother.

**PHILEMON
8–21**

Since a slave revolt would greatly threaten Roman social and economic conditions, disobedient and runaway slaves were punished severely as a deterrent to others.

**PHILEMON
9**

on the basis of love. Christian love, not a grudging obedience to Paul's command, was the only basis on which a true brotherly relationship could be built between Philemon and Onesimus.

old man ... prisoner. While not appealing to his apostolic authority, Paul certainly appeals to the respect Philemon has for him! Paul's stress on his imprisonment (vv. 1,9,23) may be a hint that he, too, knows the limitations of a form of enslavement.

**PHILEMON
10**

my son. Onesimus became a Christian through Paul's ministry. Paul elsewhere spoke of his converts as his children (1 Cor. 4:15,17; Gal. 4:19; Phil. 2:22; 1 Thess. 2:7,11).

**PHILEMON
11**

useless ... useful. There is a play on words here. These two words, which sound very similar in Greek, share a root word that was pronounced the same way as the word for "Christ" (*christos* means Christ; *chestos* means useful). Through Christ, Onesimus (whose name means *useful*), formerly a useless, disobedient slave, has now become truly useful as a brother in the Lord.

PHILEMON 12

In spite of his love, Paul had to send Onesimus back since harboring a runaway slave was a serious crime. The reality of his conversion would be seen in his willingness to return to Philemon and face up to the consequences of what he had done. Christian slaves were expected to view their work for their master as working for the Lord (Col. 3:22–25). This does not mean that Christianity condones slavery as a legitimate institution, but, given the social order of the time, this was a way for individual Christian slaves to express their loyalty for Christ within the limits imposed upon them.

PHILEMON 16

as a man and as a brother in the Lord. Literally, "in the flesh and in the Lord." "In the flesh" Onesimus is just a slave, but "in the Lord" he is now Philemon's spiritual brother.

PHILEMON 17

partner. While Paul does not request Philemon to release Onesimus from slavery, ultimately it is this vision of love and equality between all Christians that undermines the oppression of slavery, economic oppression, or social injustice.

PHILEMON 18

Onesimus may have stolen some money before running away. Besides that, his escape caused economic loss through lost services.

PHILEMON 19

with my own hand. Paul most generally wrote the body of his letters through a secretary (see Rom. 16:22), but then he often wrote personal notes at the end of his letters with his own hand (see also 1 Cor. 16:21; Gal. 6:11; Col. 4:18; 2 Thess. 3:17). Here, writing with his own hand is probably a reassurance that he will pay Philemon back for his financial losses.

10

notes

Giving Real Support

Prepare for the Session

	READINGS	REFLECTIVE QUESTIONS
Monday	Job 2:11–12	How often have you been willing to leave the comfort of your home to go comfort a friend?
Tuesday	Job 2:13	How comfortable are you just sitting and being silent with a sorrowing friend?
Wednesday	Job 6:14	Who has been there to help you at times when you felt estranged from God? How did they help?
Thursday	Job 6:15–20	Reflect on a time when you felt disappointed in your friends. What can you learn from this about being a friend?
Friday	Job 6:21	What fears do you have that keep you from truly being a friend?
Saturday	2 Timothy 4:16–17	Have you ever felt God giving you strength when no human friend supported you?
Sunday	Philippians 4:14–19	What have you done to show your thanks to friends who supported you when you needed them?

11

BIBLE STUDY
- to learn what it means to be emotionally supportive in a relationship
- to look at the support Job needed in his life, as well as the successes and failures of his friends to provide that support
- to acknowledge our own need for emotional support and to consider how to get that support

LIFE CHANGE
- to analyze our own experience in troubled times
- to interview a couple of our friends about difficult times they have gone through
- to ask our pastor for the name of a fellow Christian going through difficulties who might enjoy a visitor

Icebreaker

10-15 minutes

**GATHERING
THE PEOPLE
⟡ Form
horseshoe
groups of 6-8.**

Friend or Enemy? Everyone in the group should pick from the following list three ways to finish the sentence: "If you want to be my friend ..." Mark them with a ✔. Then when everyone is finished sharing, each person should pick three ways to finish the sentence: "If you want to be my enemy ..." using the same list. Mark these with an **X**.

- ☐ serve me liver and onions
- ☐ dress like I do
- ☐ play rock music on the radio
- ☐ laugh at what I say
- ☐ put lots of garlic on my spaghetti
- ☐ call me by my nickname
- ☐ take me to a health food store
- ☐ play country music on the radio
- ☐ ask my mom to show old photos of me
- ☐ buy me tickets to the opera
- ☐ give me a week with just my kids
- ☐ buy me tickets to a football game
- ☐ take me camping in the mountains

Information to Remember: In the spaces provided, take note of information you will need as part of this group in the weeks to come.

PEOPLE:

1. A person in the group (besides the leader) I learned from this week was:

2. A person who lifted my spirits was:

EVENTS: An event that is coming up that I want to make sure I am part of is _____. It will be _____ (time) on _____ (date) at _____ (location).

And if I have time, I would also like to be part of _____. It will be _____ (time) on _____ (date) at _____ (location).

LEARNING FROM THE BIBLE

Bible Study

30-45 minutes

The Scripture for this week:

JOB 2:11–13;

¹¹*When Job's three friends, Eliphaz the Temanite, Bildad the Shuhite and Zophar the Naamathite, heard about all the troubles that had come upon him, they set out from their homes and met together by agreement to go and sympathize with him and comfort him.* ¹²*When they saw him from a distance, they could hardly recognize him; they began to weep aloud, and they tore their robes and sprinkled dust on their heads.* ¹³*Then they sat on the ground with him for seven days and seven nights. No one said a word to him, because they saw how great his suffering was.* ...

6:14–21

¹⁴*"A despairing man should have the devotion of his friends, even though he forsakes the fear of the Almighty.*
¹⁵*But my brothers are as undependable as intermittent streams, as the streams that overflow*
¹⁶*when darkened by thawing ice and swollen with melting snow,*
¹⁷*but that cease to flow in the dry season, and in the heat vanish from their channels.*

11

[18]Caravans turn aside from their routes;
they go up into the wasteland and perish.
[19]The caravans of Tema look for water,
the traveling merchants of Sheba look in hope.
[20]They are distressed, because they had been confident;
they arrive there, only to be disappointed.
[21]Now you too have proved to be of no help;
you see something dreadful and are afraid."

...about today's session

A WORD
FROM THE
LEADER

1. What was Walter Winchell's definition of friendship? Do you agree or disagree?

Write your
answers
here.

2. Where does the leader suggest many people have found friends who are supportive? Have you found your best friends in these groups? If not, where have you found true friends?

Identifying with the Story

U **In**
horseshoe
groups of 6–8,
explore
questions as
time allows.

1. If you were to choose three friends to come and be with you while you were going through hard times, who would you choose and why? (You can choose people you actually know, famous people, or fictional people.)

2. What is the closest you have come to going through a time of despair like Job was going through?

3. Who or what helped you get through the time you referred to in question 2?

today's session

What is God teaching you from this story?

1. What three things did Job's friends do well at the beginning of this story?

   _____

   _____

   _____

2. What is a benefit of weeping with a friend?

3. What is the essence of what Job's friends did wrong?

4. In what New Testament stories does Jesus refute the idea that people who suffer are more sinful than others?

   _____

   _____

5. What is the main thing we should consider when we support a friend?

Learning from the Story

In horseshoe groups of 6–8, choose an answer and explain why you chose what you did.

1. Had you been one of Job's friends in this story, what would you have done or said to help him?

2. Job compared his friends to unreliable, intermittent streams that ceased to flow in the dry, hot season. What would you compare your friends to?

   ☐ the same—intermittent streams
   ☐ more like a dry river bed that hasn't seen water in years!
   ☐ what friends?
   ☐ a deep, cool, refreshing mountain stream
   ☐ a deep river—but totally polluted!
   ☐ other:_____

11

3. Job said, "A despairing man should have the devotion of his friends, even though he forsakes the fear of the Almighty" (6:14). What do you see as the most important thing a friend can do for someone who is struggling with God?

life change lessons

1. Name some tragedies where a person might need a supportive friend. Include those listed in the session, as well as others you think of.

2. What temptation should be avoided when listening to a person going through hard times?

Caring Time

15-20 minutes

During this time, have everyone in the group finish the sentence: "The thing I could most use the support of friends in dealing with right now is ..." Go around the group and have each person pray for the person on his or her right, using the Prayer/Praise Report and concerns listed. Start with this sentence:

"Dear God, I thank you for my friend _____."

Close by thanking God for bringing you together as a group and by asking Him to give you the strength and wisdom to be a supportive friend.

Pray specifically for God to guide you to someone to invite next week to fill the empty chair.

Reference Notes

Use these notes to gain further understanding
of the text as you study on your own.

JOB 2:11   ***all the troubles that had come upon him.*** These included loss of his livestock, servants, and finally his children in a series of catastrophes (Job 1:6–22). Then he developed a painful skin disease (Job 2:1–10).

JOB 2:12   ***could hardly recognize him.*** This could have been from the disfiguring aspects of the skin disease or from the effects of his deep mourning.
tore their robes and sprinkled dust on their heads. These acts were traditional signs of mourning in this culture (see Lam. 2:10; Matt. 26:65).

JOB 2:13   ***sat on the ground.*** This was another sign of mourning (see 2 Sam. 12:16).
seven days and seven nights. Since creation was finished in six days, seven was considered to be a number of completion.
No one said a word. They had enough understanding to realize that sometimes when a person is mourning, what he or she needs most is the quiet presence of friends. They understood what Solomon later wrote in Ecclesiastes, that there is "a time to be silent" (Eccl. 3:7b). Unfortunately, they then started talking, and undid their good work! They blamed Job's misfortune on him, saying it must be some kind of punishment for unrighteous behavior (see esp. 4:7–9; 8:4–7; 11:13–20).

JOB 6:14   ***though he forsakes the fear of the Almighty.*** A person of faith should not turn away from a friend who has turned from God. Such action would probably only harden the person even more against God. Sticking by a person in such a time may be God's way of bringing the individual back to Him. In fact, Job had not turned against God. However, he was saying that even if that were to happen, his friends should stick by him.

JOB 6:15–17   ***as undependable as intermittent streams.*** In a dry land like Israel, a reliable source of water was vital. But many streams, called "wadis" were formed by mountain run-off in the spring and then dried up in the hottest part of the summer when they were needed the most. Job was saying that his friends were like such wadis. When things "heated up" for him, they were not true friends. In Isaiah 48:18, God similarly promises that the peace He gives will be as reliable as a river, rather than an unreliable wadi.

JOB 6:20   ***they had been confident.*** They thought they were okay because they knew where water was, having seen it before. But when they came to the place where the water had been, the stream had dried up. Job felt like he had similarly relied on friends, thinking they would be there for him, but they weren't.

11

notes

Showing Real Confidence

Prepare for the Session

	READINGS	REFLECTIVE QUESTIONS
Monday	2 Timothy 1:1–4	Which of your friends do you remember in prayer on a daily basis?
Tuesday	2 Timothy 1:5–6	Which of your friends' gifts are you encouraging, and which of them are you looking at with jealousy or envy?
Wednesday	2 Timothy 1:7	Reflect on whether you are approaching life with timidity or the power, love, and self-discipline God is prepared to give you.
Thursday	2 Timothy 1:8	Do you have friends or companions you are ashamed of when you are out in public? How can you change that shame to encouragement?
Friday	2 Timothy 1:8–12	How willingly do you take on the suffering that sometimes comes with standing up for Christ?
Saturday	2 Timothy 1:12	How firmly convinced are you right now of the reality of Jesus Christ?
Sunday	2 Timothy 1:13–14	Whose faith can you look to as a pattern for your own spiritual life?

12

BIBLE STUDY

- to look at the confidence that Paul showed in Timothy and how we can express the same confidence in our relationships
- to better understand how important it is that others show confidence in us
- to discover how best to express confidence in a genuine, uncontrived way

LIFE CHANGE

- to teach a child a new skill this week and give him or her a chance to use that skill
- to identify a younger person in our church to whom we can teach a task or ministry that we have traditionally done
- to identify a person in our church or family who seems to lack confidence and share with that person what Paul wrote to Timothy

Icebreaker

10-15 minutes

**GATHERING
THE PEOPLE
○ Form
horseshoe
groups of 6–8.**

Child Prodigies. For each of the categories below, pick someone from your group you think might have been a "child prodigy" by excelling in that area. Everyone in the group should be assigned by the group to one of the categories. Then each person should share how appropriate the group's judgment was to their childhood experience.

_____ smuggling stray animals into the home

_____ having and surviving childhood accidents

_____ making up imaginative excuses for misbehavior

_____ talking at an early age

_____ climbing the highest trees in the neighborhood

_____ watching horror movies without having nightmares

_____ inventing imaginative games that the other children wanted to play

_____ going through the most new clothes in a year

Information to Remember: Finish the following sentences as you look around at the people here today.

1. A person here I would like to get to know better is:

2. A person in this group who has really been a blessing to me during these sessions is:

Bible Study

30-45 minutes

The Scripture for this week:

LEARNING
FROM THE
BIBLE

2 TIMOTHY
1:1–14

¹Paul, an apostle of Christ Jesus by the will of God, according to the promise of life that is in Christ Jesus,

²To Timothy, my dear son:

Grace, mercy and peace from God the Father and Christ Jesus our Lord.

³I thank God, whom I serve, as my forefathers did, with a clear conscience, as night and day I constantly remember you in my prayers. ⁴Recalling your tears, I long to see you, so that I may be filled with joy. ⁵I have been reminded of your sincere faith, which first lived in your grandmother Lois and in your mother Eunice and, I am persuaded, now lives in you also. ⁶For this reason I remind you to fan into flame the gift of God, which is in you through the laying on of my hands. ⁷For God did not give us a spirit of timidity, but a spirit of power, of love and of self-discipline.

⁸So do not be ashamed to testify about our Lord, or ashamed of me his prisoner. But join with me in suffering for the gospel, by the power of God, ⁹who has saved us and called us to a holy life—not because of anything we have done but because of his own purpose and grace. This grace was given us in Christ Jesus before the beginning of time, ¹⁰but it has now been revealed through the appearing of our Savior, Christ Jesus, who has destroyed death and has brought life and immortality to light through the gospel. ¹¹And of this gospel I was appointed a herald and an apostle and a teacher. ¹²That is why I am suffering as I am. Yet I am not ashamed, because I know whom

12

I have believed, and am convinced that he is able to guard what I have entrusted to him for that day.

¹³What you have heard from me, keep as the pattern of sound teaching, with faith and love in Christ Jesus. ¹⁴Guard the good deposit that was entrusted to you—guard it with the help of the Holy Spirit who lives in us.

...about today's session

A WORD FROM THE LEADER

Write your answers here.

1. Many people feel they must have gifts like _____, _____, or _____ to contribute in a meaningful way.

2. How can we show confidence in someone without being phony?

Identifying with the Story

⊌ In horseshoe groups of 6–8, explore questions as time allows.

1. Who passed faith on to you? Was it a parent or grandparent, as with Timothy, or a friend or teacher? What did this person say or do that was most influential?

2. Paul affirmed Timothy's gifts. What are some of the gifts others have said they see in you?

3. What would it mean for you to "fan into flame" the gifts you mentioned in question 2?

   ☐ to use them more
   ☐ to develop them more through training
   ☐ to use them for God, instead of just secular work or personal need
   ☐ to have more confidence in them
   ☐ other:_____

1. Why is it important for athletes to show confidence in their teammates?

2. In what two qualities of Timothy did Paul express confidence?

   _____

   _____

3. How did Jesus respond to His disciples when they asked that He increase their faith?

4. What might a Christian who lacks confidence in his or her gifts really need?

5. How would Paul's words about God's power have helped increase Timothy's confidence?

6. What were some ways Paul showed confidence in Timothy through his actions?

7. What position does tradition say Timothy eventually filled?

12

Learning from the Story

In horseshoe groups of 6–8, choose an answer and explain why you chose what you did.

1. From reading this part of Paul's letter to Timothy, how confident would you say Paul was in Timothy as a disciple?

   ◆ · ◆

   not at all   a little   mixed   quite confident   totally confident

2. If you were Timothy, which of the things Paul said would do the most to increase your confidence?

   ☐ Paul's affirmation of my faith (v. 5)
   ☐ Paul's reminder that the Holy Spirit is the source of my gifts (vv. 6–7)
   ☐ Paul's reminder that success doesn't rest on my ability but on the power and grace of God (vv. 8–10)
   ☐ Paul's own firm confidence in Christ (v. 12)

3. Why do you think Paul expressed these thoughts to Timothy?

   ☐ to help him feel better about himself
   ☐ to spur him on to even greater things
   ☐ to set him up to do Paul a favor
   ☐ to flatter him in order to keep Timothy on his side
   ☐ other:_____

life change lessons

How can you apply this session to your life?

Write your answers here.

1. What is a parent saying to a child when he or she does the child's science project?

2. We need to show confidence in people through both _____ and _____.

Caring Time

CARING TIME

⚲ Remain
a horseshoe
groups of 6–8.

During this time, have each person in the group finish the statement, "An area where I could use more confidence is ..." Then pray that God will strengthen your group members in the areas they mentioned. Also, use the Prayer/Praise Report and pray for the concerns listed.

Pray specifically for God to guide you to someone to invite next week to fill the empty chair.

Reference Notes

**BIBLE
STUDY
NOTES**

Use these notes to gain further understanding
of the text as you study on your own.

**2 TIMOTHY
1:1**

an apostle of Christ Jesus. At first glance it is surprising that Paul uses his title in such a personal letter. However, as in 1 Timothy, he is making his appeal in this letter as an apostle. This time his appeal is to Timothy. Paul urged him in strong terms to maintain his loyalty to him and the gospel, despite the suffering this may entail. There may be a second reason Paul uses his title. This letter would probably be read by others. In particular, Timothy would need to show it to the elders in Ephesus when he told them that Paul wanted him to leave and go to Rome.

**2 TIMOTHY
1:3**

I constantly remember you. Paul prayed regularly, and in those prayers he always remembered Timothy.

**2 TIMOTHY
1:4**

Recalling your tears. Paul is probably remembering when they parted the last time, he to go on to Macedonia while Timothy stayed in Ephesus (see Acts 20:37 for a similar situation).
I long to see you. This is the main reason Paul wrote this letter, to urge Timothy to join him (see 2 Tim. 4:9).
joy. Once again, as he did in Philippians, Paul sounded a note of joy even though he was in prison.

12

**2 TIMOTHY
1:5**

Eunice. Timothy's mother was a Jewish Christian (see Acts 16:1). His father was a Gentile (a Greek), who probably was not a believer.

fan into flame. "Rekindle." Paul uses the image of a fire, not to suggest that the gift of ministry has "gone out," but that it needs constant stirring so it always burns brightly.

the gift of God. Paul reminded Timothy not only of his spiritual roots (the faith of his mother and grandmother), but of the gift (*charisma* in Greek) he was given for ministry.

timidity. Some people are naturally more shy than others, and Timothy was probably more shy than the outspoken Paul. Paul said that even a shy person does not need to be ruled by timidity or fears in regard to acting for Christ because God empowers us to do more than we would be able to do naturally.

power/love/self-discipline. The gift the Spirit gave Timothy led not to "timidity" but to these positive characteristics.

ashamed to testify about our Lord. The gospel message about a dying Savior was not popular in the first-century world. The Greeks laughed at the idea that the Messiah could be a convicted criminal and that God was so weak He would allow His own Son to die. And the Jews could not conceive of a Messiah (whom they knew to be all-powerful) dying on a cross (which they felt disqualified Him from acceptance by God). It was not easy to preach the gospel in the face of such scorn.

ashamed of me. When Paul was rearrested, his friends deserted him (see 2 Tim. 1:15). He did not want Timothy to do the same.

his prisoner. Paul may have been in a Roman jail, but he knew he was not a prisoner of Caesar. He was, and had long been, a willing prisoner of Jesus (see Eph. 3:1; 4:1; Philem. 1,9).

join with me. In fact, rather than being ashamed of the gospel (or of Paul and his suffering), Timothy ought to share in his suffering.

suffering. Paul understood from his own experience (and that of Jesus) that suffering is part of what it means to follow the gospel (see Rom. 8:17; 2 Cor. 4:7–15; Phil. 1:12,29; Col. 1:24; 1 Thess. 1:6; 2:14; 3:4; 2 Tim. 3:12).

has saved us. Timothy could face suffering because he had already experienced salvation. This was an accomplished fact.

grace. God's work of salvation depends wholly on "grace" (His unmerited favor lavished on His creation), not on "anything we have done." This grace, which was in place from "the beginning of time," is "given us in Christ Jesus" (see Eph. 1:4).

appearing. The Greek word is *epiphaneia* (from which the English word *epiphany* is derived). It refers here to the "manifestation" of God's grace via the incarnation of Christ.

2 TIMOTHY
1:10
(cont'd)

2 TIMOTHY
1:12

2 TIMOTHY
1:14

death/life. Jesus' work of salvation is described in His two-fold act of destroying the power of death over people (death no longer has the final word) and bringing resurrection life in its place.

I am not ashamed. The fact that he was in prison brought no shame to Paul, despite how others viewed it.

In words paralleling verse 12 and 1 Timothy 6:20, Paul urged Timothy to preserve faithfully the "sound teaching" of the gospel.

12

notes

Understanding
Real Greatness

Prepare for the Session

	READINGS	REFLECTIVE QUESTIONS
Monday	Matthew 20:20–21	If you could ask Jesus just one favor, what would it be?
Tuesday	Matthew 20:22–23	What "cup" or common experience of hard times have you shared with a friend? How has that affected your friendship?
Wednesday	Matthew 20:24	When have you done something that made your friends indignant?
Thursday	Matthew 20:25	Have you in any way tried to "lord it over" your friends lately? How?
Friday	Matthew 20:26–27	What have you done in the past few weeks that was an act of service to one of your friends?
Saturday	Matthew 20:28	Reflect on the love Jesus had for you when He gave His life for you.
Sunday	Philippians 2:3–11	Reflect on the love it must have taken for Jesus to leave His place in heaven and take on the humble form of a human.

BIBLE STUDY
- to discover what true greatness means from a Christian perspective
- to understand how striving for the secular meaning of greatness can destroy relationships
- to appreciate how the greatness that comes through servanthood enhances relationships

LIFE CHANGE
- to analyze how we are serving others through our work
- to get involved in one ministry through which we can serve others in a way that is meaningful to us
- to take a new look at the "servant" tasks we do, particularly in our own families

Icebreaker

10–15 minutes

GATHERING THE PEOPLE ♘ **Form horseshoe groups of 6–8.**

Bullish on People. Over the past few weeks, we have "invested" in each other as a group. What kinds of investments have various group members turned out to be? Look at the list below and find a person in this group who best fits each category. Share these with each other in a spirit of affirmation.

_____ **Blue-Chip Stock**—the reliable one, performing steadily and truly

_____ **Growth Stock**—the one who has grown and "shot up" the most during these sessions

_____ **Passbook Savings**—not flashy, but steady, reliable, and always available to the group

_____ **Precious Metals**—the one showing his or her inherent (self) worth

_____ **Commodity Futures**—the one showing a lot of potential for growth beyond this group

_____ **Mutual Fund**—the one with diverse strengths that contributed to the group

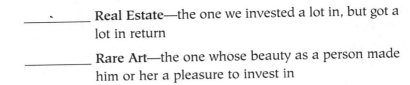

_____ Real Estate—the one we invested a lot in, but got a lot in return

_____ Rare Art—the one whose beauty as a person made him or her a pleasure to invest in

Information to Remember: Finish the following sentences as you look around at the people here today.

1. A person in the group I would like to hear from more today is:

2. A person God may be leading me to say something special to today is:

Bible Study

30-45 minutes

The Scripture for this week:

²⁰*The mother of Zebedee's sons came to Jesus with her sons and, kneeling down, asked a favor of him.*

²¹*"What is it you want?" he asked.*

She said, "Grant that one of these two sons of mine may sit at your right and the other at your left in your kingdom."

²²*"You don't know what you are asking," Jesus said to them. "Can you drink the cup I am going to drink?"*

"We can," they answered.

²³*Jesus said to them, "You will indeed drink from my cup, but to sit at my right or left is not for me to grant. These places belong to those for whom they have been prepared by my Father."*

²⁴*When the ten heard about this, they were indignant with the two brothers.* ²⁵*Jesus called them together and said, "You know that the rulers of the Gentiles lord it over them, and their high officials exercise authority over them.* ²⁶*Not so with you. Instead, whoever wants to become great among you must be your servant,* ²⁷*and whoever wants to be first must be your slave—*²⁸*just as the Son of Man did not come to be served, but to serve, and to give his life as a ransom for many."*

...about today's session

1. What are some of the ways our culture defines greatness?

2. What are some of the destructive effects of our culture's definition of greatness?

Identifying with the Story

⚘ In horseshoe groups of 6–8, explore questions as time allows.

1. How does the mother of James and John compare to your own mother?

   ☐ My mother would never have been so brazen.
   ☐ My mother would never have gone out of her way for me like that.
   ☐ I can see my mother doing the exact same thing.
   ☐ My mother wouldn't have asked—she would have demanded!
   ☐ My mother wouldn't have encouraged such ambition.
   ☐ Other:_____

2. Had you been one of the other disciples, what would have been your reaction to their behavior?

   ☐ I would have been upset I hadn't thought of it first.
   ☐ I would have understood their ambition.
   ☐ I would have felt smug because of their failure.
   ☐ I would have resented their attempt to "climb the ladder" at my expense.
   ☐ I would have been sad that they let ambition threaten our fellowship.
   ☐ Other:_____

3. When has someone's ambition (yours or someone else's) come between you and your friends or coworkers?

1. What factors might have given James and John a claim to a high position among the disciples?

2. What view of the Messiah did James and John and the other disciples assume?

3. What did Jesus say His disciples would have done if His kingdom were of this world?

4. Whom did Jesus tell His disciples would be first among them?

5. What three people are mentioned who could be considered "great" by Jesus' definition of greatness?

   _____

   _____

   _____

6. What is one of the biggest problems with a secular definition of greatness?

13

Learning from the Story

In horseshoe groups of 6–8, choose an answer and explain why you chose what you did.

1. Why were the other 10 disciples upset with the 2 brothers?

   ☐ They didn't have the courage to speak for themselves—they went to Mommy!

   ☐ The brothers were trying to outmaneuver them in a power game.

   ☐ The brothers were only concerned about themselves after Jesus had spoken of His impending death.

   ☐ They didn't think the brothers were worthy of such positions.

   ☐ Other:_____

2. What would you say is the essence of Jesus' response to the two brothers here?

   ☐ Christians shouldn't have ambition.

   ☐ Service, not power, is the way to get ahead.

   ☐ Stop thinking of self and start thinking of others.

   ☐ Christian leaders should be team-builders, not autocrats.

   ☐ Other:_____

3. Right now, as you relate to those around you, where are you on the following scale?

   1 · 2 · 3 · 4 · 5 · 6 · 7 · 8 · 9 · 10

   a claw-my-way-to-the-top   a Christlike
   autocrat   servant

life change lessons

How can you apply this session to your life?

Write your answers here.

1. Finish this sentence: "Authentic Christian relationships are modeled after _____."

2. What are we advised to take on in the spirit of Christ?

Caring Time
15-20 minutes

Pray for the concerns listed on the Prayer/Praise Report, then continue with the evaluation and covenant.

1. Take some time to evaluate the life of your group by using the statements below. Read the first sentence out loud and ask everyone to explain where they would put a dot between the two extremes. When you are finished, go back and give your group an overall grade in the categories of Group Building, Bible Study, and Mission.

 GROUP BUILDING

On celebrating life and having fun together, we were more like a ...
wet blanket ································· hot tub

On becoming a caring community, we were more like a ...
prickly porcupine ···················· cuddly teddy bear

 BIBLE STUDY

On sharing our spiritual stories, we were more like a ...
shallow pond ······················· spring-fed lake

On digging into Scripture, we were more like a ...
slow-moving snail ···················· voracious anteater

 MISSION

On inviting new people into our group, we were more like a ...
barbed-wire fence ···················· wide-open door

On stretching our vision for mission, we were more like an ...
ostrich ····························· eagle

13

2. What are some specific areas in which you have grown in this course?

☐ affirming and encouraging others
☐ using my life experiences to help others
☐ being mentored and/or mentoring an emerging leader
☐ developing a daily quiet time with God
☐ finding a way to use my gifts and talents in a ministry
☐ developing a habit of studying the truths of the Bible to help me with life change
☐ other: _____

A covenant is a promise made to another in the presence of God. Its purpose is to indicate your intention to make yourselves available to one another for the fulfillment of the purposes you share in common. If your group is going to continue, in a spirit of prayer work your way through the following sentences, trying to reach an agreement on each statement pertaining to your ongoing life together. Write out your covenant like a contract, stating your purpose, goals, and the ground rules for your group.

1. The purpose of our group will be:

2. Our goals will be:

3. We will meet on _____ (day of week).

4. We will meet for _____ weeks, after which we will decide if we wish to continue as a group.

5. We will meet from _____ to _____ and we will strive to start on time and end on time.

6. We will meet at _____ (place) or we will rotate from house to house.

7. We will agree to the following ground rules for our group (check):

☐ **PRIORITY:** While you are in this course of study, you give the group meetings priority.

☐ **PARTICIPATION:** Everyone is encouraged to participate and no one dominates.

☐ **RESPECT:** Everyone has the right to his or her own opinion, and all questions are encouraged and respected.

☐ **CONFIDENTIALITY:** Anything said in the meeting is never repeated outside the meeting.

☐ **LIFE CHANGE:** We will regularly assess our own life change goals and encourage one another in our pursuit of Christlikeness.

☐ **EMPTY CHAIR:** The group stays open to reaching new people at every meeting.

☐ **CARE and SUPPORT:** Permission is given to call upon each other at any time especially in times of crisis. The group will provide care for every member.

☐ **ACCOUNTABILITY:** We agree to let the members of the group hold us accountable to the commitments which each of us make in whatever loving ways we decide upon.

☐ **MISSION:** We will do everything in our power to start a new group.

☐ **MINISTRY:** The group will encourage one another to volunteer and serve in a ministry, and to support missions by giving financially and/or personally serving.

13

Reference Notes

Use these notes to gain further understanding
of the text as you study on your own.

MATTHEW 20:20

the mother of Zebedee's sons. In this society, women were of little worth, and thus we have this description where the mother isn't even named and where the sons are "Zebedee's" sons. In Mark's account, James and John approached Jesus directly. Regardless of the role their mother played in this incident, it is clear that they were held responsible for it (v. 24). In accordance with the general assumption about the Messiah, the disciples expected that Jesus would come into a position of authority as the new king of Israel. Those who sat on His right and His left would be His chief lieutenants. James and John were thinking in these terms in spite of the fact that Jesus had just announced His coming death (Matt. 20:17–19).

MATTHEW 20:22

drink the cup. This phrase means to share the same fate. In the Old Testament, drinking the cup is a metaphor for experiencing God's wrath (e.g., Ps. 75:8; Isa. 51:17–23). Here, the cup refers to Jesus' suffering and death for the sins of the world.

We can. In spite of their bold assertion, they did not grasp what He meant. They probably assumed He was referring simply to being willing to share in His future, which they imagined would be one of power and prestige.

MATTHEW 20:24

they were indignant. As self-serving as the request of James and John had been, the response of the others was not much better. All 12 share the view that the kingdom would be earthly and political, with Jesus as the reigning king and them as his chief lieutenants.

MATTHEW 20:26

servant. Rather than becoming masters (and exercising authority), they were to become servants and meet the needs of others. The Greek word for *servant, diakonos,* from which the English word *deacon* is derived, became the most common description of church leaders in the early church.

MATTHEW 20:28

ransom. This is not meant to be understood in terms of a strict legal transaction in which Jesus died to somehow buy off either God or the devil, a debate that engaged theologians in times past. Instead, *ransom* was a word generally used to describe the act of freeing people from bondage, whether through the literal payment of a purchase price or through some act of deliverance.